UNLEASHING THE POWER OF BOLD WOMEN ENTREPRENEURS

SASSY,
Classy
&
BADASSY!

HANNA OLIVAS
ALONG WITH 12 BADASS WOMEN

ISBN: 978-1-964619-15-6

TABLE OF CONTENTS

INTRODUCTION

Welcome to *Sassy, Classy, and Badassy,* a vibrant anthology that celebrates the essence of bold women entrepreneurs who have rewritten the rules of success. This book is a tribute to the fearless spirit, unshakable confidence, and transformative vision of women who have dared to step out of the conventional mold and carve their own paths in the world of business.

Within these pages, you'll embark on an inspiring journey through the personal and professional lives of trailblazing women who have turned their dreams into thriving enterprises. Each story is a testament to their resilience, creativity, and unapologetic approach to leadership. From breaking through barriers to creating groundbreaking innovations, these women exemplify the perfect blend of sass, class, and unrelenting badassery.

Through candid narratives and practical insights, our contributors share their unique experiences, offering a wealth of wisdom on overcoming obstacles, shattering glass ceilings, and redefining what it means to lead with authenticity and purpose. Whether it's launching a startup, scaling an established business, or forging new paths in their industries, these women have navigated their journeys with grace and grit, inspiring others to follow suit.

Sassy, Classy, and Badassy is not just an anthology—it's a call to action for every aspiring and established entrepreneur. It's a guide that provides actionable advice, strategic insights, and a fresh perspective on what it takes to succeed in today's competitive landscape. Each chapter serves as a beacon of inspiration, offering practical tools and motivational stories that empower you to unleash your own potential and achieve extraordinary success.

As you delve into these pages, may you find the courage to embrace your own unique qualities, the confidence to break free from conventional constraints, and the determination to build a business that truly reflects your vision. Here's to celebrating the unstoppable spirit of women entrepreneurs who prove every day that with a little sass, a lot of class, and a whole lot of badassery, anything is possible.

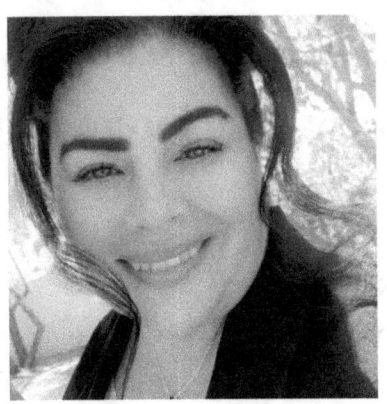

Hanna Olivas

Founder and CEO of She Rises Studios

https://www.linkedin.com/company/she-rises-studios/
https://www.facebook.com/sherisesstudios
https://www.instagram.com/sherisesstudios_llc/
www.SheRisesStudios.com

Author, Speaker, and Founder. Hanna was born and raised in Las Vegas, Nevada, and has paved her way to becoming one of the most influential women of 2022. Hanna is the co-founder of She Rises Studios and the founder of the Brave & Beautiful Blood Cancer Foundation. Her journey started in 2017 when she was first diagnosed with Multiple Myeloma, an incurable blood cancer. Now more than ever, her focus is to empower other women to become leaders because The Future is Female. She is currently traveling and speaking publicly to women to educate them on entrepreneurship, leadership, and owning the female power within.

Sassy, Classy, Badassy:
How to Thrive in Business and Life

By Hanna Olivas

In a world that often whispers for women to shrink and settle, embracing the sassy, classy, and badassy spirit is nothing short of revolutionary. It's about reclaiming your power, standing unflinchingly tall, and leaving a mark that cannot be ignored. This is not just a mindset—it's a way of life that I've lived through myself. From overcoming humble beginnings and significant health challenges to building thriving businesses, I've walked this path with fierce determination and an unwavering belief in my own strength. My story is one of trials and triumphs, and it's here to inspire and empower you to embark on your own journey with confidence and resilience.

Rising from Humble Beginnings

Growing up in a modest household, my upbringing was shaped by my single mother and my grandparents—wonderful people who never had the chance to graduate high school. They gave me all the love they could, but their lack of formal education was a constant reminder of the obstacles that lay ahead. Despite these challenges, I never let them define me. Instead, they fueled a burning desire within me to prove that greatness could emerge from even the most unassuming beginnings.

I remember the feeling of dreaming big in a world that seemed set on keeping me small. I was determined not just to survive but to thrive. My drive wasn't just about escaping the confines of my circumstances but about building a life where I could fully express who I was meant to be. With relentless hard work, a fierce sense of self-belief, and a vision for a future that went beyond my immediate reality, I charted a path to success. This journey was never easy, but every step forward was a testament to my commitment to my dreams.

Overcoming Health Challenges

Life, as it often does, threw me a curveball when I was diagnosed with multiple myeloma—a form of cancer that shook my world to its core. This diagnosis was more than just a health scare; it was a test of my mental, emotional, and spiritual resilience. In that moment, I had a choice: I could let this disease define me or I could redefine how I approached life.

I chose the latter. I sought out the best medical treatments available, adopted a lifestyle that prioritized my well-being, and leaned heavily on my faith and my family. This period in my life was a crucible of sorts, transforming my health challenges from mere obstacles into opportunities for personal growth. My health became not just a priority but a profound aspect of my journey. Instead of viewing it as an insurmountable barrier, I saw it as a chance to cultivate a deeper understanding of my own strength and resilience.

Building Businesses from the Ground Up

Managing my health while building multiple businesses from scratch was no small feat. Each venture came with its own set of challenges, but every setback was met with a resolve to learn and adapt. Today, I own several businesses that each bring in seven figures—testaments to my commitment to integrity, innovation, and a deep desire to make a positive impact on others' lives. These businesses are not just financial successes; they are embodiments of my values, creativity, and leadership.

Each business is a piece of my vision—an extension of my passion for creativity and a reflection of my commitment to helping others succeed. The road wasn't always smooth, but every hurdle was an opportunity to refine my approach, learn new lessons, and grow stronger. This journey taught me that resilience and determination are not just traits but essential tools for anyone aiming to build something meaningful and lasting.

Leading with Heart and Mind

As the Chief Branding Officer of She Rises Studios and FENIX TV, and through my involvement in initiatives like the InspireHER project and the Lift series, I've made it my mission to inspire and uplift women across the globe. These roles allow me to blend creativity, leadership, and a deep-seated passion for positive change. Each day, I get to contribute to a larger vision—one where women are empowered to rise, lead, and make their own mark.

My work in these roles isn't just about professional success; it's deeply personal. It's about creating spaces where women can find their voice, connect with their purpose, and thrive. It's about building platforms that amplify their stories and successes. The heart of this work is rooted in my own experiences and the belief that every woman has the potential to be extraordinary.

Embracing the Qualities of Sassy, Classy, and Badassy

Owning Your Voice and Authenticity

To be sassy is to be unapologetically yourself. It's about embracing your true essence and standing firm in who you are, regardless of external expectations. For me, this meant letting go of societal norms that tried to shape me into something I wasn't. It meant celebrating my quirks and strengths and living authentically.

In my personal life, being sassy has meant letting my true self shine through. It's about having the courage to express my opinions, share my passions, and live in a way that feels true to who I am. This authenticity attracts genuine relationships and opportunities. When you show up as your true self, you build deep and meaningful connections.

In business, authenticity builds trust. It's about being transparent and real, which in turn attracts loyal clients and partners. My businesses reflect my values and vision because they are built on the foundation of authenticity. When you are true to your principles, you create a brand that resonates deeply with your audience.

Your health journey should also be approached with authenticity. Understand your body, listen to its signals, and make choices that align with your well-being. For me, this meant creating a balanced approach to diet and exercise, incorporating mental health practices that supported my lifestyle, and being honest with myself about what worked and what didn't. Emotional and spiritual authenticity is about acknowledging your true feelings and beliefs. It's a continuous journey of self-discovery, faith, and personal growth.

Cultivating Grace and Elegance

Being classy is about embodying grace and elegance. This doesn't mean being aloof or detached; it's about treating others with kindness and respect, regardless of their status or background. In my personal life, I strive to approach every interaction with empathy and composure. It's about being the best version of yourself and lifting others up along the way.

In business, classiness translates to professionalism and integrity. It's about conducting yourself in a way that earns admiration and respect. My approach to business is rooted in ethical conduct and treating everyone—whether team members, clients, or competitors—with the utmost respect. This not only builds a positive reputation but also fosters strong, trusting relationships.

Approaching your health with grace means making sustainable, healthy choices rather than resorting to quick fixes or extreme measures. It's about respecting your body and honoring it with the care it deserves.

Classy emotional and spiritual health involves maintaining inner balance and managing stress with poise. Practices like mindfulness, meditation, and prayer have been essential in helping me stay grounded and focused.

Harnessing Inner Strength and Resilience

Being badassy is about tapping into your inner strength and resilience. Life will inevitably present challenges, but it's your response that defines you. I've faced numerous obstacles, from health issues to business setbacks, but each time I chose to rise stronger. Resilience is about cultivating a mindset that sees challenges as opportunities for growth and learning.

In business, being badassy means taking risks, thinking outside the box, and embracing failure as a stepping stone to success. My ventures grew because I wasn't afraid to innovate and adapt. Each failure was a lesson, each setback a chance to refine my approach. Embracing this mindset has been crucial in pushing my businesses to new heights.

Your health journey will have its ups and downs, but being badassy means persevering through the difficulties. It's about setting goals and pursuing them with unwavering commitment. For me, this meant staying dedicated to my treatment plan, exploring new health strategies, and maintaining a mindset that sees every obstacle as an opportunity for growth. The process can be challenging, but it's through resilience that you discover your true strength.

Emotional and spiritual strength comes from within. It's about having faith, staying positive, and believing in yourself even in the darkest times. I found strength in my faith and the support of my family, which helped me navigate the toughest moments. Surround yourself with positivity and embrace your emotions as part of your growth journey.

Growing Together in Confidence

Building confidence is not a solitary endeavor; it involves creating an environment where you and those around you can flourish. One of the most important aspects of growing in confidence is building a strong support network. Surround yourself with people who believe in you, challenge you, and encourage you to reach your potential. My journey would not have been possible without the unwavering support of my family, friends, and mentors. Their belief in me, especially during difficult times, has been a cornerstone of my strength.

Confidence also comes from continuous learning and competence. Invest in yourself through ongoing personal and professional development. Attend workshops, read extensively, take courses, and stay curious. The more you learn, the more confident you become in your abilities. Seek out mentors and role models who inspire you and can offer guidance. Embrace lifelong learning as a fundamental aspect of your growth.

Set clear, achievable goals for yourself and work diligently towards them. Each milestone you reach boosts your confidence and motivates you to aim higher. Celebrate your successes, no matter how small, and use them as stepping stones toward your bigger dreams. Every accomplishment is a reflection of your hard work and dedication.

Taking care of yourself is essential for building confidence. Prioritize self-care activities that rejuvenate your mind, body, and soul. Whether it's indulging in a spa day, engaging in a workout, or enjoying a quiet evening with a book, make self-care a priority. It's not a luxury but a necessity for maintaining your well-being and confidence.

Four Ways to Be Sassy, Classy, and Badassy

Be Bold and Fearless

Being bold means stepping out of your comfort zone and taking risks. Whether it's pursuing a new career, starting a business, or making a significant life change, don't let fear hold you back. I've taken many bold steps throughout my life, each one leading to new opportunities and growth. Embrace uncertainty as a part of your journey and let it drive you toward greatness.

In business, boldness is crucial. It's about innovating, challenging the status quo, and making strategic decisions. I've launched new ventures, taken calculated risks, and pushed my businesses to new heights. Boldness in business can lead to remarkable success and set you apart in a competitive market.

Being bold in your health means advocating for yourself, exploring new approaches, and refusing to settle for mediocrity. I've sought out top treatments, tried alternative therapies, and made significant lifestyle changes to enhance my health. Your well-being is worth fighting for and being proactive in seeking solutions will lead to better outcomes.

Bold financial decisions can lead to significant wealth growth. Invest wisely, take calculated risks, and explore new opportunities. I've built my wealth by being strategic, informed, and bold in my financial choices. Don't let fear of the unknown limit your financial potential.

Being emotionally and mentally bold involves confronting your fears, seeking help when needed, and pushing yourself to grow. I've faced my fears head-on, sought therapy, and continuously worked on my emotional and mental well-being. Boldness in this area leads to profound personal growth and resilience.

Spiritual boldness is about exploring your beliefs, questioning, and finding your own path. My spiritual journey has been one of exploration, faith, and continuous growth. Be bold in seeking what nourishes your soul and remain true to your spiritual path.

Cultivate Grace and Dignity

Grace and dignity in life involve treating others with kindness and respect, regardless of the circumstances. It's about being composed and respectful, even in challenging situations. I've aimed to live with grace and dignity, building strong and respectful relationships along the way.

In business, grace and dignity translate to professionalism and ethical conduct. Treat everyone—colleagues, clients, competitors—with respect. Conduct yourself with integrity, and you will earn respect and trust. My businesses have thrived because of the grace and dignity with which I approach every interaction.

Approach your health journey with grace. Respect your body, listen to its needs, and make choices that honor your well-being. My health journey has involved making respectful, dignified choices that align with my body's needs and limitations. Every decision regarding your health should reflect self-respect and care.

Handle your finances with grace and dignity. Be responsible, make informed decisions, and treat money with respect. I've built and maintained wealth by managing my finances with dignity. Financial management should reflect your values and aspirations.

Embrace Authenticity and Resilience

Authenticity is about staying true to yourself despite external pressures. Embrace your individuality and let it shine through every aspect of your life. In business, authenticity builds trust and attracts genuine connections. I've learned that being authentic creates a brand that resonates deeply with its audience.

Resilience is crucial in overcoming life's challenges. Cultivate inner strength and a positive mindset to navigate obstacles. Each setback is an opportunity for growth and learning. Embrace challenges as stepping stones to greater achievements.

Foster Continuous Growth and Empowerment

Personal and professional growth is a lifelong journey. Invest in yourself through continuous learning, skill development, and self-reflection. Empower yourself by setting and achieving goals that align with your passions and values. Surround yourself with mentors and peers who inspire and support your growth.

Conclusion: Your Sassy, Classy, Badassy Journey

Embracing the sassy, classy, and badassy spirit isn't about fitting into a mold; it's about creating your own path and celebrating the qualities that make you uniquely powerful. It's about rising above challenges, owning your worth, and striving for excellence. By embracing these principles, you transform not just your own life but also inspire others to do the same.

As you embark on your journey, remember that confidence, resilience, and grace are essential in navigating the complexities of life and business. Embrace your inner strength, stay true to yourself, and keep pushing boundaries. Together, we can build a world where women thrive, lead with purpose, and shine in every aspect of their lives. Your journey to being sassy, classy, and badassy starts now. Embrace it fully, and watch your life transform in ways you never imagined.

XOXO,
Stay Sassy, Classy, and Badassy
Hanna Olivas

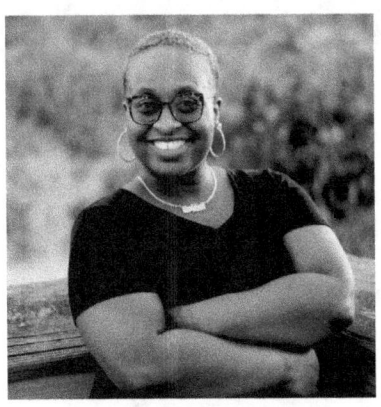

Dominique Carson

Licensed Massage Practitioner, Author, Journalist, & Orator

https://www.linkedin.com/in/dominiquemcarson/
https://www.facebook.com/dmc922
https://www.instagram.com/domcarson90
https://linktr.ee/dom0922

Dr. Dominique M. Carson, LMP is an award-winning and globally recognized freelance journalist, licensed massage practitioner, orator, and author. For over a decade, she interviewed over 100 notable figures in popular culture, such as Tito Jackson, Latto, H.E.R, Coco Jones, Jekalyn Carr, Jon B, Charlie Wilson, Regina Belle, Patti Labelle, Kirk Franklin, and many more. She also collaborated with Brooklyn historian and journalist Suzanne Spellen and launched a 118-page journal on Lefferts Manor, a neighborhood in Brooklyn. Carson also served as Program and Communications Coordinator for Man Up! Inc., a nonprofit organization in East New York, Brooklyn. While at the organization, she received a citation from the New York City Council and the "It's My Park Award" from the Partnership for Parks for community engagement in her hometown, East New York, Brooklyn. Her story has appeared in media outlets such as Sheen Magazine, Impact Magazine, Femi Magazine, Industry Times, and

Forbes.One, VoyageLA, ShoutoutLA, and Bold Journey, to name a few. Carson's overall goal is to facilitate people's lives with her hands and words.

Slaying with Sass: Embracing Your Boldness and Confidence

By Dominique Carson

A high school friend of mine, Brandon Walker, also known as Jolly Roger Boy (my mom's nickname for him because of his electrifying energy, vibrant dance moves, and upbeat energy as a master of ceremony at events), was truly the "life of the party". He once wrote in my high school yearbook in 2008, "My Domo, stay sassy, sweet, smart, beautiful, BAD (Blessed and Divine). P.S. "You're my valedictorian no matter what." When I asked B to write in my yearbook, he jokingly said, "I need some time to write in this book; I'll give it back to you when I'm done; you can wait patiently." I raised my hands and said, "Okay," and he was just one of those people that I wanted to write in the book. He gave it back to me, smiled, and said, "Domo, here you go; it takes more time to write in the book for someone who is one of the real ones."

After reading his message in my book, I thought, 'B described me very well, and from the time we were in the 9th grade, he didn't have a problem calling me a "sassy nerd." From the moment Brandon and I met in Mr. Maher's "Fitness for Life" class back in 2004, he was going to be a comical brother and friend to me, and he didn't have a problem making sure I was on my toes each time he saw me in the hallways of Edward R. Murrow High School. I think Brandon knew I was self-assured about myself and liked to empower others in various situations, and this stems from my upbringing, which embodied the likes of my mother and maternal grandmother. I did not have a problem being intelligent while getting my point across and letting others know where I stand if there are any discrepancies.

As a 14-year-old, it made me feel good because I was a bookworm with a sassy attitude. I wasn't afraid to utilize my brain, was outspoken, and knew when to be boisterous and sophisticated. To me, you can be sophisticated and sassy because you're embracing style with attitude, and your motto is to be fabulously unstoppable. Now, when I read that note 16 years later, this anecdote makes my heart smile, and I still strive to have those qualities as an adult. It was like I wasn't afraid to be the young woman who stood out to guys with various personalities, but in a good way. My personality and sass allowed me to blend in with all social groups in high school; I was literally a chameleon.

I also remembered when Brandon told me that I was going to speak at our high school friend, the late Anita P. Bhimsen's wake, when she died in January 2018. In his eyes, it wasn't an option, but he said, "Dom, you have the personality and demeanor to speak at her wake and represent on behalf of our high school." See, it all goes back to being sassy and memorable because people are drawn to those who value class and sass, which is why their aura is so memorable.

However, due to life experiences and maturity, it's more refined, but the core, the inner essence of me, is still sassy. I would rather be known as sassy and classy rather than indifferent, despondent, tasteless, or inelegant. It was the roots that were planted in me at an early age. The women in my family, paternal and maternal, made it crucial to present yourself like a lady and know how to make an everlasting impression on others. My grandmother used to say to me and my other female cousins, "Princess, you never know who is watching you, so be mindful of how you carry yourself in the street."

At 33, I am still unafraid to be different and express myself uniquely; it's a way for me to positively stand out from everyone else. I strongly believe this is one of the reasons why my grandfather called me the "Quiet Storm." I know when to be sassy, classy, assertive, and establish boundaries so no one steps on my toes. My mother, also known as my Ladybug, would tell the family not to underestimate my oldest daughter. She knows how to be sassy and sarcastic when necessary, though her demeanor is calmer, but she has a temper that can be explosive when provoked. My grandfather described my temper as a burner that gradually intensifies, making, it hard for me to calm down once it reaches its peak. Most of the time, I am laid-back, easy-going, mellow, and mild; that's my demeanor. However, I can be stern to ensure no one takes advantage of me or mistakes my kindness for weakness. It's imperative, as a sassy woman, to be assertive so I can effectively communicate my thoughts.

As I continue to slay with sass, I show that I need to blend grace with wit to create a memorable and engaging presence. Over the years, I have demanded respect from peers, family, friends, and an intimate lover while maintaining a poised attitude. I added my clever spin because I knew I had to be as sharp as a tank. I remember a defining moment when I introduced my sassiness in school. Transitioning to junior high school, I demanded respect from two educators who were pompous and conceited and did not like the fact that they had a student who was not afraid to challenge them in the classroom. As a child, I loved math, but there was a math educator who didn't appreciate students questioning his teaching methods. As a result, he would lower my grades, citing "disorderly conduct." It was frustrating because, at times, I felt like I was punished for being smart instead of embracing my eagerness and desire for math. To make matters worse, during parent-teacher conferences, my parents and the principal asked the teacher if I was rude, disrespectful, cut class, or disruptive, and his response was "No." His antics were worse, and by the end of the school year, I transferred to another school because my parents believed I wasn't being challenged at all as a student. I didn't have a problem with the change because I needed to surround myself with an academic institution that would push me immensely as a student.

There was another instance where I needed to present my sass in the 8th grade after my mother had a conversation with my English teacher.

I had a teacher in junior high who was an excellent teacher but could be arrogant. For the first marking period, he mixed another student's and my name, and we didn't even belong in the same class. Before he realized he made a terrible mistake, he said on my report card, "I wasn't going to class, wasn't doing homework, gave me Cs, and said I didn't initiate effort in class." I kept explaining to my family, especially my mother, that those grades were not mine; it was a mix-up. My mother still had her reservations, but once we entered the classroom to see my teacher and opened his grade book, he said the name "Dominiqua Jackson," and my mother went ballistic. She said," That's not my daughter's name; you could've gotten her in a lot of trouble because of your careless mistake." To top it all off, Dominiqua and I were not in the same class, and he still couldn't get the grades right. My mother apologized to me and my grandmother and gave me quite a shopping spree that weekend. When I saw my teacher on Monday, I let him have it because I take my schoolwork seriously. His attitude about the error was emphatic when he realized he made a mistake but it was too late. I told my teacher that I was about to accept the death sentence and be breathless, meaning my mother's punishment. Thankfully, I had enough courage to stand up to the educator, trust my instincts, and follow my parents' advice about staying on top of my affairs.

On the other hand, being sassy, classy, and a badass may have its' challenges and disadvantages **IF** it's not regulated. You must be balanced and filled with gratitude; otherwise, you will come off as standoffish, rude, arrogant, and egotistical. It can be misinterpreted with these negative characteristics, leading to further conflicts, isolation from groups or events, and a strain on your relationships, whether intimate or personal. Others may feel like they're not being respected, that you're intentionally belittling them, and that you're not willing to adapt by being receptive to others. You do **NOT** want to be a woman who is known for being offensive and disruptive because your sassiness is construed as insubordinate and starts to diminish your credibility.

When you start to rely on your sassiness, it can become evasive, and you're becoming emotionally unavailable. For a long time, I did not want to be vulnerable, although I didn't have a problem being empathetic to people I trusted in my life. But, I realize that vulnerability is a form of strength, and crying is a form of cleansing. You just have to make sure that you can trust the people around you. Otherwise, they will take your kindness for weakness. I strive to make sure that once I invest in someone emotionally, business, or personally, I have the ability to present depth, and you're not so eager to present quick wit and you're being sincere. If sass is not presented correctly, it will look like you want to be confrontational, cynical, constantly sarcastic, or dismissive. Yes, you want to be confident and outspoken, but make sure your sass doesn't overshadow your persona.

Over the years, I have blended my savviness and sassiness, and it has been a spectacular combination. It shows people that your demeanor is knowledgeable and assertive at the same time. It is such a great combination, especially for a woman like me who likes to solve problems. I am eager to navigate challenges with wisdom and wit to make a difference in people's lives, especially as a massage therapist. As a massage practitioner, I can present my scholastic knowledge to my clients while still being myself, and they will feel comfortable around my presence. It is such a gratifying feeling because I am effective with my communication while enhancing their massage experience. I can utilize my massage strokes and techniques to soothe their bodies, minds, and souls while relieving stress. I appreciate that I can understand and connect with clients on a deeper level, which makes the massage sessions more therapeutic. Each time I massage my client, they trust my touch and expertise to sedate their sympathetic nervous system and enhance their health and overall well-being.

Ladies, you can be bold and boisterous, but you have to be balanced. Balance does not mean short-changing your personality; it just needs to be regulated and better managed with the outside world. I would advise my ladies to be sassy when it's time or when the situations are appropriate. When you have this frame of mind about sass, it can lighten the mood without being cantankerous, or it can add value to the conversation. Deciphering the time to be sassy is also based on reading your room or setting because you don't want people to be uncomfortable. Then, you don't want to be animated with your sass because it will come off as unauthentic, and you're going overboard. After a while, people are now tiresome and completely unphased by your sassiness because it comes off as pretentious, forced, staged, and disingenuous. As you continue to balance your sass, you know when it's time to shift gears and be serious about having meaningful conversations with people, and you're well-rounded as a communicator.

I encourage all my ladies to embrace their flair because they possess an instinctive aptitude for doing their best and being their best. It is one of the best things about being sassy - making a decision to be savvy and sharp-witted. I strive to make the best decisions, even when they are difficult or necessary. I **LOVE** being a sassy, classy, and badassy woman because I have the ability to exercise my intellect and mental agility while staying true to myself and not conforming to societal standards of a woman. As a sassy woman, I aim not to sugarcoat anything for people, especially my nearest and dearest, but my words must be delivered responsibly. I do not have time to be a wolf in sheep's clothing; I am a proud lioness, and you will hear me roar when necessary. My grandfather used to say that the best charm you can give anyone, especially the opposite, is to be yourself because you're being genuine and have no false pretenses. It also allows people to build trust in you because, even though your responses may be sassy at times, you're still being transparent. This makes you a more dynamic and captivating person to be around on a daily basis because you know how to be elegant, confident, polished, and sophisticated. By incorporating all these elements, you are embracing your individuality and will continue to feel empowered truthfully. Although it may be intimidating at times for some, you're consciously doing your best, not short-changing yourself, and encouraged to be unapologetic about your sassiness. However, with age and experience, a sassy, classy, and badassy woman doesn't always need to respond because silence can be louder, and your presence can speak volumes. I am embracing the refined version of myself while staying true to my roots. When you merge sass and elegance, it becomes timeless with every step you take, and every move you make. It's up to you to present your bold and lively spirit to everyone.

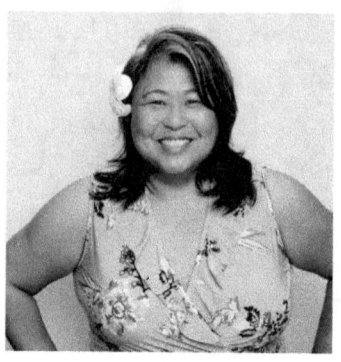

Gemma Bulos

Founder and CEO of The Reinventor Lab

https://www.linkedin.com/in/gemmabulos
https://www.facebook.com/gemmabulos
https://www.instagram.com/gemmabulos
https://www.gemmabulos.com
https://www.thereinventorlab.com/

Gemma draws on her vast experience as a multi-award-winning social entrepreneur, global speaker, educator, musician, movement builder, and filmmaker to catalyze change in the world. Recognized globally for her expertise in imposter syndrome and designing for social impact, she supports purpose-driven start-up founders, coaches, and business owners to improve the world AND make money. Gemma won Best Social Entrepreneur in Asia award from the World Economic Forum; has delivered hundreds of talks in 36 countries (including 3 TEDx) alongside Nobel Peace Laureates and world leaders; and taught Social Entrepreneurship at Stanford University. Despite her extraordinary achievements, Gemma grappled with imposter syndrome throughout her life, driving her to develop proven tools for overcoming it. She coaches emerging change agents worldwide, empowering them to amplify their impact and visibility by establishing thought leadership and adopting agile, sustainable business practices. Visit gemmabulos.com to explore how Gemma can help future-proof your business and career.

A Single Drop Starts A Wave

By Gemma Bulos

It's hard to imagine that my mission, which has provided over 1 million people with clean water and sanitation in Asia and Africa all started with the song "We Rise."

How did I get here?

In 2001, I was a preschool teacher and a professional jazz singer in the bustling streets of New York City. By day, I would serenade my young students with "Old MacDonald Had a Farm," and by night, I'd let loose scatting to "I'm in the Mood for Love"!

It was one fateful incident that set me on an unexpected path to discover my true purpose. On a sobering Tuesday, September 11, 2001, I made the selfish decision not to go to work. I wasn't sick, just apathetic. Little did I know, I narrowly avoided being in the basement of the World Trade Center when the tragic events unfolded, on my way to teach my preschool class.

That day became a turning point as I realized that my life would be changed forever. When I look back at my life now, it's the incident that marked my transformation - before 9/11 and after 9/11- from self-serving to servicing the world. Suddenly, aspirations of becoming the next EGOT Winner (Emmy, Grammy, Oscar, Tony) were not the top dream on my vision board. I was forced to start asking myself a different question: What am I going to do with this second chance when others were not so lucky?

I did what my heart told me to do and I channeled my feelings into a song called "We Rise." The song embodied the idea of people uniting and rising together from tragedy. My brain somehow shifted from what I could do for myself to be famous to what I could do for all people to thrive. It's amazing how much more open and creative your brain can be when you are searching for meaning.

In this new rewired state where my brain and heart were working together to live on purpose, I had this far-fetched idea of mobilizing what I called The Million Voice Choir to sing We Rise from all over the globe in celebration of peace and unity. I made the bold, seemingly irresponsible, and irrational decision to leave everything that kept me in a state of 'want', giving away all my possessions, and setting off with just my guitar and a backpack to explore what it felt like to be in a state of 'service'. I began traveling the world with the little money I had, inviting people to join me in this global peace movement.

Can it be done?

This dream was unprecedented. No one had ever done it before. Facebook was still just a college connection platform, email was not mainstream yet (hello AOL, Hotmail, and Earthlink!), and there were still some tech failures like Myspace and Friendster to overcome before social media evolved into our dominant way of connecting through Twitter, Instagram, and TikTok. To get strangers to join an unknown vagabond's peculiar mission to build a million voice choir, I had to tap into some serious sassy, classy, and badass energy to keep me connected and driven to achieve this goal!

I embraced my sass by being bold and maintaining an unwavering belief that my vision was not only possible, but achievable. I embodied class by empathizing with others, forging deep connections, and wholeheartedly supporting their dreams. And I unleashed my inner badass by taking action, even when fear and uncertainty loomed large.

By living these principles, something magical happened. People were not only moved by the song, message, and mission, they joined in! They self-organized all over the planet, recruited singers and non-singers, learned the song, and hosted their own peace events. And on one day - September 21, 2004, choirs in over 100 cities in 60 countries sang "We Rise" from all over the planet in celebration of the United Nations International Day of Peace.

Looking back, I can see why the movement resonated. It was right after 9/11 and people wanted to be part of something bigger and express how important it was to foster peace in the world. I can also see why the message connected deeply. It revolved around the idea that a single drop of water can start a wave. This served as an invitation for people to recognize their own power, and everything they say and do can have a ripple effect impacting everything around them. People became that drop. They unleashed the power within them to raise their voice, unite their community, and connect to a shared vision with other people around the world.

Interestingly, because of that metaphor, I became affectionately known as the "water lady". I was even invited to sing at the United Nations Water for Life Conference, where I learned about the global water crisis. I was shocked to find out that 1 in 7 people lacked access to safe water and contaminated water was one of the highest causes of illness and death in the world.

The impact of water (or lack of it) runs deep. Former UN Secretary-General Kofi Annan said "The human right to water is indispensable for leading a life in human dignity. It is a prerequisite for the realization of other human rights." The statistics that stopped me in my tracks highlighted how women and girls suffer the most from the lack of access to water and sanitation. They are primarily responsible for fetching water and doing water-related chores like cleaning, cooking, washing, and bathing. Especially with the current effects of climate change, women and girls can spend up to 8 hours a day fetching water, carrying back about 40 pounds of water, and facing the risk of injury or violent attack due to the difficult terrain.

What does this mean? It means women lack opportunities for livelihood and are unable to be productive, earn money, or secure employment. For girls, it means missing out on education. About one in ten girls drop out of school at the age of 13 because there are no proper water and sanitation facilities in schools, and they have no place to clean themselves during their periods. It was hard for me to comprehend that the lack of water has such a huge impact on the lives of women and girls - their health, education, security, status, and more.

After building the choir, I asked myself again - what can I do to be of service to the world? I listened to what my heart needed me to do, and this time, the answer was obvious. I needed to focus on uplifting women around the globe so they have opportunities to thrive - and that was by training them to bring sustainable water services to their villages. I continued to travel around the globe and had the honor of meeting and supporting remarkable women who, inspired by our shared mission, unearth their own power to transform their lives and uplift their communities.

During my research, I discovered that the United Nations Food and Agricultural Organization found that excluding women from decision-making processes in water and sanitation planning led to a high rate of failure in those initiatives. This puzzled me since women are the ones most affected by water issues, and have the most at stake. Studies have shown that women have strong entrepreneurial spirits due to limited access to the formal labor force. It was evident that our mission would be to train and empower women to create their own water and sanitation solutions, allowing them to take control of their water resources without having to rely on external assistance. It was crucial to involve women in decision-making processes as they are most invested in finding sustainable water solutions.

Take, for example, Auntie Josie from Siasio, a remote village in the mountainous region of the Philippines. After mobilizing the choir, I learned simple water technologies that could be built anywhere in the world, even by people like me who had no construction or engineering background. I was lucky enough to receive a $10,000 award from Queen Latifah and Covergirl for Women Changing the World Through Music and founded an organization called A Single Drop for Safe Water in the Philippines. I met Auntie Josie because her community received funding to build a water system. Due to our organization's expertise in helping communities design their own solutions, the funders brought us in to support them.

During the project design process, the community found that one water spring could service two villages, providing hundreds of people with access to clean water. However, the spring was located on private property, so permission from the landowners was needed. This is where Auntie Josie came in. She was a retired principal and elementary school teacher and probably knew every person in the community because she had engaged with them at some point in their education. Being involved in the planning process from the beginning, she understood how crucial it was to get access to the water spring for both communities. With her community knowledge and connections, she was able to convince the landowners to provide access to the water and even hand over ownership of the spring to the villages. This was a HUGE accomplishment, but there was still another major obstacle. The owner's house was built on top of the spring! Auntie Josie took action, and mobilized the two communities to help dismantle the house, move it to another location, and rebuild it. The water system was constructed, and Auntie Josie was elected as the president to manage it.

Then there's Grace Mushongi from Bukoba, Tanzania. She participated in a training program organized by my second water organization, Global Women's Water initiative, I co-founded in Sub-Saharan Africa. We train women to become water technicians, trainers, and social entrepreneurs. They learn to build technologies such as rainwater harvesting systems, toilets, and filters. The training also equips them to educate others about hygiene practices and to become entrepreneurs by selling their services and products to generate income.

Initially, when Grace first attended our training that brought together village women from three countries in East Africa, she was shy and didn't interact much because she felt intimidated due to her educational background - she never finished middle school. However, she surprised everyone by excelling in all the skills she learned at our training. When she went back home, she raised funds, and led other women in her communities to build five tanks to capture and store rainwater - all within six months. Grace became known as the local water hero for her efforts in promoting hygiene practices and sharing water-related knowledge in her community. Her success inspired others, including the husbands of her friends, many of whom asked her to teach their wives the skills she had learned.

And finally, there's Fiona from Naivasha, Kenya. For 14 years, she was a commercial sex worker. Her husband had left her with two children and sex work was the only way she could make money to take care of her family because, like Grace, she also did not graduate from secondary school. When she arrived at one of our trainings, she said she was stunned and excited to see our trainer - another woman. Not only was our female trainer building tanks, but she was teaching other women how to do it!

Fiona totally immersed herself in the training and picked up all the skills very easily. She was a natural. It was very clear to our trainer how eager, committed, and competent Fiona was. Our trainer took Fiona under her wing, made sure she had all her questions answered, and made sure she mastered masonry and construction skills. As a result, Fiona was able to leave her work as a commercial sex worker because she got offered a job to be a Water Sanitation and Hygiene expert in her community. Her transformation was remarkable.

I feel a profound connection with these women and their journeys. It's as if we are kindred spirits. Like me, they discovered their purpose in service, challenged traditional beliefs, and unlocked the sass, class, and badass power that lay dormant within them, waiting to be awakened. None of us embarked on this path thinking, "I'm going to bring clean water and sanitation to a million people in Asia and Africa," or "I'm going to convince a former student to donate their water spring to two surrounding villages," or "I'm going to rise above my circumstances, become a mason, and transform my life." We didn't make such grand declarations. Our impact began when we listened to our hearts and acted on what it needed us to do. It was when we unleashed the potential within ourselves, started believing in what we formerly believed was not possible, and took bold action, that the true change began. Like removing a dam holding back billions of gallons of water, we released a dormant force of sass, class, and badass spirit, believing audaciously that we could change our lives, our circumstances, and without even knowing it, the world.

I invite you to consider: What sassy thing can you do today? What bold, audacious dream do you have, and what would your life look like if you achieved it? What classy act can you perform this week? Who can you connect with deeply to help achieve your dream? And what small but badass step can you take that will bring you 1% closer to your goal? By embodying and unleashing your sassy, classy, and badass selves, you are already making an impact. Be that drop of water, and make waves!

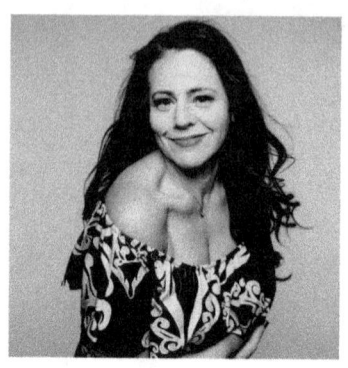

Jennifer Day

Founder and CEO of FAB Approach (Jennifer Day, LLC)

https://www.facebook.com/profile.php?id=100092556880826
https://www.instagram.com/fabapproach/
https://checkya.com/fabapproach
https://www.jenniferdayllc.com/

Jennifer is a Transformative Emotional Balance & Armor Coach, an Author & Speaker. She specializes in working with emotionally resistant clients to find self-love, clarity, boundaries, and power aimed at releasing their emotional "Weight of Armor." Jennifer has overcome personal challenges of self-abandonment, corporate burnout, Neuroendocrine cancer surgery, and managing her neurodivergent conditions. After releasing 125 pounds, she realized the importance of addressing underlying issues, including childhood trauma, to achieve lasting success.

Her mission is to meet clients where they are and guide through life's big challenges and changes with processes, expertise, intuition, authenticity, integrity, and grace. She facilitates awareness for clients to experience transformative change and growth, not "fix" them. Through the process, clients become curious and gain the awareness that anger, anxiety, indecision, people-pleasing, & even extra weight can be released. This becomes possible by forging a path built on trust, connection, and support, to find the strength within to thrive!

From Resistance to POWER

By Jennifer Day

It's funny how you think you've got all your shit together, and then suddenly, you have a WTF moment! Like, what? I had this "thing" covered already, didn't I? I've done a ton of work, had a lot of growth, and things are good. Right?!

For those who wonder why they don't see themselves like they used to, keep reading. It's called "Life Happens" or as a good friend says "Life is Life-ing." As women tend to do, we nurture and care for others, often forgetting that we cannot pour from an empty cup. The important thing to remember is that we do not do ourselves or anyone else a service by putting our needs last. The key is to give from an overflowing cup, which I'm sure just made most of you giggle a bit. I'm serious, though; your energy and capacity to handle life are so much stronger when you take care of yourself first.

In being 100% transparent, I have not always done my best with this. Most of my life, including being a single parent and pretty much every relationship, was about putting others first. I generally found that I would anticipate the needs of others in hopes that they would reciprocate my efforts. Most people did not, hardly ever anyway. Expectations are the easiest and fastest way to be disappointed. The best way to combat that is through using agreements. We'll cover that later.

For now, let's focus on the topic of this chapter. I've been on a fairly intense healing journey since September 8, 2022, when I was laid off from my corporate construction position. When I got the call, I had just finished walking with a girlfriend on my hometown green, asking her advice on how to transition from proving my worth in a world of chaos to massage and energy work.

Just before COVID hit in 2020, I graduated as a Licensed Massage Therapist in Florida, and then the world kinda stopped. Well, not for healthcare workers or construction workers who built hospitals needing those patient beds. Yuppers, you guessed it, I worked for a mechanical contractor who was building a 90-patient bed wing in Tampa, FL. There was no break coming; we had a letter giving us permission to cross the local bridges to come to work.

Once that project was 90% complete, I was moved on to our next hospital project in St. Petersburg, FL. It was during this project that I would become a patient at that very same hospital where a bronchoscopy would reveal a golf-ball-sized Neuroendocrine Tumor blocking 85%-90% of the main airway to my left lower lung in October 2020. It turns out that this cancerous tumor had been growing for about 5-7 years. Coincidence that I lost my Mom in 2015, and the lungs are where we hold grief? I think not! There was another small tumor in my right middle lobe, just sitting in the tissue. Mind you, I had been told prior to all of this that I had asthma. (Always advocate for yourself when something doesn't feel right!)

I had to go to another hospital to have the surgery completed in February 2021. That is another story for another day. Recovery went as smoothly as it could for the 6-weeks that my ADHD brain would allow me to sit still. I clearly remember the first time I walked up and down my driveway, wanting to prove to myself that I had this recovery thing down, and then spent the next 3 hours passed out on the couch! Silly me. I knew that I needed to make changes. BIG changes. I was eating fairly healthy at the time, so only small changes were needed there; however, big changes were on the way, and I just didn't know it yet. I lost some weight before my surgery between the stress and anxiety of being diagnosed, extra testing, and the fear of the unknown.

During healing from surgery, my body was craving something that made me feel more like me. My renewed sense of spirit found gratitude for the gift given to me of needing to slow down & appreciate life. I found a fun, new fitness group and loved it so much that I became an instructor!

In March of 2021, I got engaged to the man that I had been living with for almost two years, who helped me through my surgery. He had also just recovered from major surgery after being knocked off a ladder and breaking his pelvis in three places. It took a year for his recovery, and during that time, I was diagnosed. I'm pretty sure the dynamics of life would have changed drastically if he wasn't injured. After a weird transition back to work, I decided to change jobs in May of 2021 for a remote position with a local GC in Tampa.

In June of 2021, I got the shock of my life when the man I was going to marry vanished eight weeks before our wedding! Yes, you read that correctly…up and left. He left half of his shit at my house, strategically packed & placed for some of it, and the rest looked like he was planning an escape with garbage bags under the bed next to a machete. Days later, I found out that I was the fifth woman that he had done this to already while his WIFE was chasing him for a divorce; he ran to an old girlfriend. And he actually had the balls to unblock me long enough to request the refund from our wedding venue and arrangement deposits. F*CK YOU, DUDE and thank you, Universe (best redirection gift ever)!!!

It took me weeks to decide to leave the house. I was in total shock, disbelief and completely questioned my ability to read people or even trust myself. I began to bury myself in my work and that was the beginning of the burnout. Work loved that I gave my everything to them and never considered accommodating the help that I had requested multiple times for that $38M project.

Needless to say, in April of 2022, I decided that I needed help with processing these HUGE emotions and unhealed trauma from the previous year. I connected with a mentor who taught me that I wasn't honoring or listening to my body. She helped me to understand that I had been in survival mode and just going through life. I quickly realized that my nervous system had been telling me all along that it did not like the places, people, or situations that we were in and that additional change was needed. I joined the 6-month container that my mentor offered as a group course. It did not take long to decide that I needed to implement some big changes. I decided it was time to part with the memories of the house I bought when I first moved to FL, so I packed my things, and it was under contract as of September 1, 2022. By mid-October 2022, I was living my best life in a little apartment at the beach and had decided to take the rest of the year off to recover. Little did I know that I'd be starting a business in a few months!

In January of 2023, I opened up Heartbeats 4 Fun & Fitness, LLC, with a few friends supporting their zones of genius after splitting off from our original group class that grew to capacity. It was created as a fun, all-inclusive cardio drumming exercise community that brought joy to many in the surrounding cities. Internal changes began to take place within the coaches group, which disbanded us by September, and I closed that location. It took a lot of effort to create, implement, and help the community. It was devastating to us coaches in choosing to close the location, and our participants were equally upset and disappointed. Good news: There are discussions in the works for pop-up events, and another location is coming in 2024!

Why did I just share this whirlwind of my life? To help you see that life is never perfect. My story didn't start in 2020; it's actually the 1970s when I was a heavy child from day one. At age 5, I'd go to Weight Watcher meetings with my Mom and Grandma. Childhood and teenage years were filled with bullying, name-calling, and feeling less than at almost every turn. Even my family would tell me, "You're such a pretty girl if you'd only lose some weight." WTH did THAT mean? I wasn't pretty until I lost weight. I know they meant well, but kids are sponges, and I was no different. That became a trauma in and of itself that I didn't start tackling until my 30s.

I have tried all kinds of ways to lose weight throughout my life. Fads, starvation, eating plans with purchased foods, and even bariatric surgery at one point, which was canceled just weeks before it was to take place (thankfully)! It wasn't until that 6-month container that I realized that much of the 60 lbs already lost was due to changing my eating habits, and the rest would become apparent from diving deep into inner work on the emotional Weight of Armor that I used to protect myself from life.

I started addressing the childhood trauma of being bullied, name-calling, my family's comments, and the pressures of adulting. I discovered that eating well and moving my body was only part of the equation, and as a result, I began to release weight. I enjoyed the process so much that I became a certified trauma-informed practitioner in April of 2023. By December 2023, I had gone from losing 62 lbs to 125 lbs. I decided it was time to share this important discovery with others and started another business where I help people uncover what holds them back in their journey of life, either physical or emotional Weight of Armor, or simply a combo of both!

Fast forward to April 2024, I was "gifted" the opportunity to attend a retreat with 14 other incredibly amazing and talented women. I had been dreaming and wanting to go since the opportunity was announced months before. I kept thinking that I would get there, that I belonged there and it would happen somehow. So when the text message was received from a wonderful friend that I would be given the chance, I talked it over with my partner and said YES! It was an easy decision as I had already started creating my business. I had some clients already and wrote an eBook in February, but how would I get my message out to the world?

You see, I am definitely a combo of my Mom (who played small her whole adult life) and my Dad (who is a sarcastic smartass with a big personality). That basically describes me as a "T"! And while various components of that combo worked throughout my construction industry career as a team member that built schools, restaurants, and hospitals … how would I translate that into helping people rebuild themselves?

The answer is: I love reading energy and helping people. I am an intuitive, compassionate healer with a smartass big personality. C'mon, I used to ride a full-dresser Harley Davidson, was in the corporate construction industry for 27 years, and I fit in just fine with the field guys and the office management..

On the first full day of this retreat, called Content Camp 3, I had a wave of unworthiness and shame, like I didn't belong there. I was surrounded by women who have well-established businesses, and were all sharing the gifts we have and could help each other with this weekend. Instead of suffering in silence, I leaned to my gift of vulnerability and shared my emotions and sensations with the group. I was met with the most compassionate and encouraging responses. That safe place was exactly what I needed at the time to allow all of that to flow through and process out of my body.

It turned out that I was not the only one who had moments of being unsure or uneasy; almost everyone did, and I was able to open the floor for all to share. I partnered up with a woman for our first content piece who had also experienced a similar childhood story of being overweight. She is an absolute goddess now in every sense of the world, so it was proof that I wasn't the only one who made huge changes to help me grow into my destiny. I had been telling her that I wasn't really sure how I came across when it came to social media and that I hoped people would understand my mission when we made our videos. Not only did she commend my ability to be real on camera, but she opened my eyes to just how much I was still using a facade to play small.

Ironically, I tip-toed my way through a bunch of the weekend exercises, initially feeling like I was going through the motions or activities. I knew that what I was doing was important and that my message was good but somehow still felt like I was watching someone else from the outside looking in. Have you ever felt that way?

What I didn't realize was that, little by little, I would complete each exercise, gaining a bit more growth and confidence with each component. I had to write a video script that I would be using to promote myself and my business, which would be professionally produced, so no half-ass attempts here! And then, I would go on to have professional photos and headshots done, plus record a guided meditation at RCA Records! For real, a big-time weekend with real, attainable goals. It was my first time doing any of these activities, and I loved every second of it!

I could feel myself growing during each of these events. Having professional hair & makeup done in the studio two days in a row was so dream-like, I can't even deny that I felt like I belonged there! Going to a professional recording studio where Dolly Parton and many others have trailblazed their way into the world was incredible and humbling. Recording my very own guided meditation was so rewarding, especially with the guidance of a wonderful director and a new life-long friend in the room for support. The recording was complete in only one take as I had it carefully planned out and followed the energy of my "day buddy" as she went first when we got there. Having the headphones and hearing my sultry, raspy voice (recovering from a cold) was even calming to me as I touched on each point for breathing and relaxing into the body.

Our last full day together included a nature walk in a local park. The sound of nature combined with the rustling of leaves and birds amongst other wildlife was soothing. This was perhaps the biggest moment of growth for me throughout this entire weekend. I have always had the ability to make people feel safe in my presence and share with me, so it came as no surprise to get that feedback from this group of women.

Each of us shared a vision for what was to come as a result of the work we had put into ourselves and our businesses that weekend. It was here that I declared that I would let go of my resistance and step into my power! Grief came over me and I cried. Then came tears of joy. Throughout my time to share, I wavered between excitement and being scared.

Up until that point, I was hanging onto a portion of my old life. The life that I didn't exactly love but it was like a safety blanket and it was predictable. I knew the ins and the outs. I was in between missing my old industry where I knew how to do my job inside and out, probably even in my sleep, and this new entrepreneurship stuff does not have a traditional checklist with step-by-step instructions.

Sounds like freedom, doesn't it? Well, my short answer is yes and no. Yes, to the fact that no one was pushing me for deadlines anymore or piling on more work than I could handle on any given day. And no, to the fact that no one was pushing me for deadlines or piling on more work than I could handle. LOL. If I wanted to work 10, 12, 14 hour days, I can now do that for myself and my benefit only.

I admitted to my group that compliments were something that I loved, and yet I often did not allow myself to genuinely receive them. Our mentor opened the floor to anyone who wished to share a compliment with me, and I was to only use the two magical words "thank you" without returning with a compliment. That proved to be a bit of a challenge at first, but by the second or third, I was getting the hang of it. It felt amazing to receive and hear what a brave, authentic, vulnerable badass that all of them expressed in various ways! I felt rejuvenated and lighter, leaving the park to head back.

Later that evening, we got to see the rough cuts of our videos, and I could not express the level of pure joy that washed over me when I saw myself up on that screen. My message was clear: I looked incredible, and it showed. I wasn't feeling self-conscious at all, and that is where I shine the brightest.

Since declaring that I would officially leave ALL of my resistance behind, I moved into my power of requesting the Universe to bring me those who are in alignment with me and who need my help.

Through the many years of helping others, I've learned that **everyone** has a story and deserves to feel seen, heard, and loved…which, of course, starts with YOU! I cannot stress this enough: the most important relationship you'll ever have in this lifetime is the one with yourself. I chose me, and I want you to choose yourself, too!

My mission is pretty simple, yet not easy at all. Lasting change and growth comes from addressing and healing what makes you tick at your deepest levels. I choose to help as many people as I possibly can to understand and release their emotional Armor. I believe you are meant to THRIVE, not just survive your way through life, and your body can show you the way.

It took me having an experience of sitting in a chair for hair and makeup and then slipping into one of my favorite outfits, showing off my curves, to now be comfortable with the word classy. Yes, me, classy! With the lifetime of things that I have been through, I already knew that I was sassy long before my red hair indicated that in our society! And the badass part, well, has been sprinkled throughout the chapter and beyond.

It takes a village at every point in your life, and I'm elated to have found many members of my tribe and village within the last year. And remember that it does ebb and flow as your journey of growth continues. Letting people come and go through life's lessons is not always easy; however, trying to control people to stay when they are not meant to will become that much harder for you to heal from. It's important to remember when "Life is Life-ing" and you can revisit your healing levels over and over as if they were layers of an onion. You ARE healing at each layer.

Let's move you in the direction of finding the best version of yourself amongst your tribe and village, too! Your opportunity to expand your Tribe to include me is just around the corner, so let's embark on your transformative journey together.

My resistance to not fully show up was holding me back for more than 30 years of my life and now that information and vulnerability has become my gift/MY POWER to help others! **Now I invite you to get curious about where your resistance is and let's turn it into YOUR POWER!**

With love, gratefulness, and blessings to you all!
xoxo Jenn

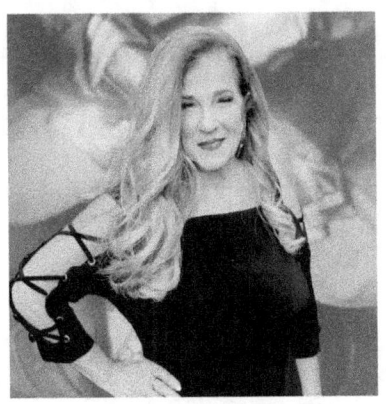

Karen Rudolf

Tranquil SOULutions, LLC
Empowerment Coach

https://www.linkedin.com/in/tranquilsoulutions/
https://www.facebook.com/karen.rudolf.14/
https://www.instagram.com/tranquilsoulutions/
www.tranquilSOULutions.com

Karen Rudolf is a transformative Life Strategist, Super Stress Reducer, and 4X International Best Selling Author. Founder of Tranquil SOULutions, she is dedicated to empowering personal and professional growth through a "W"holistic approach. With a rich background in nursing, comprehensive certifications, & licenses, Karen specializes in enhancing communication, boosting self-esteem, and fostering "W"holistic well-being decreasing stress. Her work not only shifts perceptions but also nurtures resilience and peace, making her a trusted guide in life's journey.

She can be reached at http://www.tranquilSOULutions.com Click the link and receive a complimentary gift from Karen.

From Imposed to Empowered: Crafting Your Own Story of Sass and Class

By Karen Rudolf

I never saw myself as 'bad-assy' until someone pointed it out to me! "Wow, Karen, you're one of the strongest people I know; how do you do what you do?" Say what???? Me? This had me pause and reflect on my life. We all have stories and experiences that shape us into who we are BE-coming.

I have always viewed myself as overwhelmed, stuck in a victim mentality, constantly asking "Why me?" I was a people pleaser from the start; my mother labeled me as sickly due to my asthma, making me feel like I couldn't function like everyone else. What was wrong with me? I felt 'normal', able to do everything other kids could do! Being labeled was detrimental to many of us growing up!! As a result, I lived a sheltered life, not knowing how to break free. Asthma was preventing me from fully embracing life and living it to the fullest. At six years old, I was a very curious child. Everything was a Wonderland for me. I had so many questions that my dad would often tell me, "Go out and play. You ask too many questions, so leave me alone."

This message seemed to convey that kids should be seen and not heard; what's wrong with me? Was I not supposed to ask questions? Despite this, I remained curious and frustrated. I would stomp off to my room or outside to pout, eventually becoming a loner, lost in my thoughts and imagination.

Living at the end of a street that bordered a forest, I'd go on my loner retreats into nature, seeking solace. During one of my wanderings, I found a bush that resembled an igloo, a safe haven from my parents' arguments. I would hide there with my Barbie dolls, covering them with leaves and caring for them. Even then, I knew I was a healer.

Being the curious and studious person I was becoming, I sat in the front row of my first-grade classroom. We were given a cigar box filled with what seemed like an enormous number of alphabet tiles and asked to spell out words on the blackboard. OK, I realize I'm aging myself here now, so bear with me.

I went to work on the assignment. I recall, raising my hand, to the teacher, who resembled Snow White with her long, straight blond hair, and beautiful smile, for help when I ran out of tiles. Despite my seriousness, she laughed causing the whole class to join in. I was stunned and frozen in place.

She came over to my left side, put her hand on my shoulder, and pointed to the blackboard on the back side. I had to turn my body completely around to the right side as everyone continued laughing. As she pointed to the board that read 'Happy April Fools' Day,' I just looked at it blankly.

I had no idea what April Fools' Day was or what it meant. My parents never played that game! It was at that moment, I wanted to crawl under the table. I was so humiliated. I did not get their joke and did not understand why everybody was laughing so loud, long and hard. They were laughing at me! At that moment I decided I must be stupid, and I will *never* open my mouth again.

Fast forward. I went through my schooling career with the teachers asking for answers to questions, calling on me where I'd cower whether I knew the answers or not. My response was always, "I don't know" "I don't know" became my default moving forward. Thank goodness I was relatively good on exams and able to pass my classes.

This later translated into not feeling worthy, not feeling enough. The stories we tell ourselves! Life is about cause and effect. One thing begets another, begets another until we feel as if we are spinning out of control with no way out. Victimizing!

Being a by-product of my parents, my mother's conversation was always around lack, not being enough, or not being worthy. Through no fault of her own, she didn't know what she hadn't known and probably learned it from her parents or experiences. I'm certain I picked up quite a bit from her without realizing what was going on. My 'not knowing's translated into further feelings of being stupid and unworthy, which translated into even more levels of unworthiness.

Unbeknownst to myself, I began seeking evidence that I, Karen, was indeed "stupid" and unable to do things because I didn't know how. By default!

What we focus on expands. I reached a point where I would cower when I was asked a question, becoming a people pleaser, and later beating myself up for giving away my power.

Life is about breathing without thought, basic survival skills are innate: eating shelter, and seeking love and acceptance.

Human nature innately craves to be seen, heard, loved and understood. We often seek these basic needs outside ourselves, not feeling heard, I became a people pleaser to be seen. "Here I am, look at me!!! 'Look what I did for you,' thus teaching ourselves that it's about others, forgetting about ourselves and forgetting about self-love, worthiness, and putting on our oxygen mask first.

I was Classy, Sassy and certainly Bad-Assy by looking for love in all the wrong places, my picker was not on the mark, to say the least. Being a people pleaser, just created more and more heartache and more questions of self-worth, what was wrong with me? What was wrong with my picking abilities?

I married for love and gave up my nursing career to raise the family, as I was told, my mother-in-law, before me had. 'Yes, sir, how high, sir!' Not that it was terrible, not at all being a people pleaser, it became easier and easier for me to put others first.

I hid behind my children in a very challenging relationship. I shut down. Lost my identity in the mix. When things got rocky to the point of despair, I didn't have the where-with-all to open my mouth and ask for what I wanted and needed.

I turned it over to God. I recall the day I was shoveling horse manure over my shoulder frantically; dear God if this marriage isn't supposed to be, the only way I see out of it was for him to have an affair…. Lesson learned: Be careful what you wish for! This gave me an excuse to file for divorce. I loved the idea of what I imagined 'family" was 'supposed' to look like. My self-imposed expectations, broke my heart.

When asked what I'd do after, would I go back into nursing as it was a reputable career, I recall listening to others' opinions long enough. Although nursing served me well, it also reminded me of my youth of not being heard and not being enough once more.

As I questioned the Doctors for sending patients home with scripts, I'd ask, 'Why are you masking the symptoms rather than getting to the root causes?'…. "Shut up and do your job"! I despised not being seen nor heard and I'd cave or cower.

Not knowing the direction of my future, being a single mom of 3 small children, I panicked and victimized myself to the point of a pity party without the hats and hoopla wasn't a fun place to be. Which way do I go? Dang, I could barely make a decision back then, let alone commit. I had no idea what was next or in store for me, for us. Fear prevailed.

At one moment in time, during the struggles with divorce and not being spoken to at all by my former husband, feeling quite alone, everything had to then go through the attorneys as the only means of communication.

I was informed we were going to court. Oh no! The judge, who I had put on a pedestal thinking he was going to determine my fate and the fate of my children, scared the heck out of me.

It had me pause and realize I was so in my pity party that I hadn't thought about the fate or future of our children, who were in the middle of all this chaos. I was their first advocate. Who was I? I decided to take on communication courses and promised myself I'd never be out of communication again. I'd learn to open my mouth and determine my own fate, or as close to it. I was becoming the Bad-Ass!

I was still that curious child, taking on Quantum Physics, and Neuro-Science and couldn't get enough info, the world became my oyster! What would I do with all this info, I had no idea, I felt guided, trusting my intuition.

Right around the time my divorce after 4 years was coming to a finality, my second horse got struck by lightning! Really Universe? I get supposedly Florida is the lightning capital of the world, but really? Not once, but twice.

Scamper, my heart and horse soul-mate, died saving another as he fell. I mourned for a long time with his passing. When Truman, a few years later, got struck by lightning, my Vet told me to put him down, 'Karen, you're going through a divorce, you have small children, it will cost a lot for his recovery, his chances would be slim, put him down." I recall getting still, closing my eyes, and after a few moments, flung them open to blurt out in his face, "No, not only will Truman survive, he will Thrive, and he and I will become catalysts for change!" He looked at me, shocked, and I felt just as shocked; where had THAT come from??? I don't know.

I had been seeking answers to the why me thing for some time… I studied world religion, looking for and seeking something outside of myself.

When I mentioned this scenario to my Spiritual Mentor, she asked me if I'd looked up the meaning of lightning strike as if everything was a sign or symbol. "No, I hadn't. I already know what it means." I am an intuitive. She asked, "What will you do with that?" I replied, " I'm not ready for that". She laughed, "Okay, let me know when you're ready!" I sighed, 'Ok, I will."

Lightning strike means being a Light in the World, a Messenger. After declaring Truman and I were going to be 'Catalysts for Change', I suppose I might as well step up. Bad-Ass me!!

As luck would have it, thank you once more, Universe. I got a call from my now hypochondriac mother, her attention-getting, victimized survival mechanism. Raising three small children on my own, listening to her go on all during the time I was exhausted doing 6 hours of car-pooling per day with three different schools, soccer, studies, and horse shows life became quite overwhelming, to say the least. That fatal day, when I hadn't heard from my mother, I knew something was up. I called and heard her slurring her words.

Dropping everything, I opened her door to find her on the floor in a fetal position. I hadn't seen my mother; I saw a small child overwhelmed by fear, wanting to be loved, heard, and understood.

She was 70 and had taken art classes. With no one to show her artwork to (hey, look at me, look what I did!!). She'd go to the doctor's office complaining of a Migraine and share her artwork with the staff, who ooh'd and ahh'd until the next week she'd finish another drawing and complain about the meds they had given her for migraine now was causing her to become nauseous.

She was on 19 medications when I found her that day on the floor. At that moment, I knew immediately. I had my lightning strike while scraping her off the floor, and I declared at that moment, 'The buck stops here! Not on my watch!' I AM that Catalyst for Change. I owned my Bad-Ass self that day!

My journey from feeling overwhelmed and undervalued to recognizing my strength was not just transformative—it was revelatory. It highlighted a fundamental truth: many of us are living stories not of our own making, trapped in narratives shaped by others' expectations and past experiences. My path led me to a profound realization: if I could rewrite my story, I could support others to do the same.

Not knowing the how-to's as I'd conditioned myself to be, I decided to choose to change that story once and for all.

I realized I wasn't stupid at all! Rather quite intelligent! I was becoming sassy for sure! If I hadn't known something, thank goodness for Google! Thank goodness for my curiosity as I set myself on an aligned path of learning the skills and strategies to empower myself to empower others. I was now on a mission. I had a path.

I hired a Coach, and although it hadn't worked out the way I'd hoped with my lofty expectations, through trial and error, I never gave up; I became clearer about who I was and what my needs and desires were until I found my aligned coaches.

Many were shocked at the idea of me spending so much money on my personal growth and educating myself. Whose life was it anyway? If I'd gone back to college, it would've cost me as much if not more! I obtained lots of certifications and licenses as a result. It wasn't to brag or prove myself worthy any longer; I felt the path was opening up before me. Opportunities were laid out, all of which aligned with who I was to become today and how I was meant to serve. I trust that!

Today, as an Empowerment Coach and Life Strategist I harness this understanding to enlighten others in peeling back the layers of imposed identities that have obscured their true selves. My approach is rooted in empathy and empowerment, developed through my own experiences of self-doubt and rediscovery. I work with clients to identify and detach from these limiting beliefs, replacing them with narratives of strength, capability, and self-worth today.

As a young child, I was fascinated with manipulative puzzles. I couldn't get enough solving quickly and eagerly awaiting the next. My grandfather, being a magician in his spare time, taught me a lot about perception and introduced me to those puzzles. Fast forward to today I am a creative problem solver.

I focus on the power of narrative. We each can author our life's script, yet too often, the pen is in someone else's hand. I guide my clients in reclaiming their narrative authority—highlighting their innate strengths that have been overshadowed by years of external labeling, self-doubt, and conditioning. I do that in a creative, playful way.

The process of detaching from these imposed identities is deeply intertwined with stress reduction. As we shed these external pressures, we not only find clarity and also peace. It's human nature to desire personal freedom. What does that look like? Many want it and have no idea what that even looks or feels like.

Once one moves from a state of constant reactivity to one of proactive self-definition. This shift not only decreases stress and its stressors, this also increases resilience, opening doors to new possibilities and paths previously obscured by self-imposed limitations.

As I teach the tools and techniques for mastering our stressors, I've come to realize Classy is a choice, it's something we step into like a new garment. We get to adorn it with the energy of who we choose to become.

Being around my horses has taught me just how intuitive, elegant, and loving horses truly are. After doing many years of trauma clearing alongside Truman being that catalyst for change, I've come to realize everything is energy. For me, the horse represents Power, Beauty, Grace, and Ease. All of the energies I wished to embody. When I teach embodiment work, I stand in my choice of Classy-ness, engaging others in what's possible for their choice of sassy as well.

As we navigate this journey together, I am not just a guide; I am a catalyst for deep, meaningful change. By focusing on empowerment through self-awareness and resilience, I help individuals not only confront their current challenges but also equip them for future obstacles, fostering a life of self-directed success and fulfillment.

This by no means that I don't have my share of angst, challenges, and struggles, I have the tools that support me in managing the stressors, such that I can take a deep breath and deal with them head-on rather than being the deer in the headlights and able to now give back through my services by teaching others the tools and strategies which will support you moving through your own with ease.

Consider not discounting or making your past mean something other than what it is.. in your past. Perhaps you were meant for something greater than yourself with your own life experiences. Look closer; you might find your gift or hidden gem within your own story.

Had I not been a curious child, asking questions, playing with manipulative puzzles, being creative, a nurse, studying world religions, communication, trauma release, coaching, etc… today I've become a renowned Catalyst for Change in the world of "W"holistic Empowerment, gracing stages, an International Best Selling Author, traveling, and presented globally.

As a Healer, I frame the Holistic aspects of life and well-being with a "W" as I believe you are a 'whole' person. Whole, complete, and perfect right here, right now. Being educated in the Mental, Emotional, Physical, and Spiritual, I am prepared to take you and yours on now all as a result of believing I wasn't enough, go figure!

I like to believe that life happens for a reason or a season. Life happens for me, not to me.

"When we change the way we look at things,
the things we look at change" —Wayne Dyer.

I love my life today! This quote by Wayne Dyer, which my brain heard as, when you change the way you look at things, the way you look at things change," (my brain perceived it the way it had) took me to South Africa against all odds making a difference in their educational system there, who would've thought. You never know what the Universe has in store for you. Be open, be willing, and be a YES to life!

These things created my Classy, Sassy, Bad-Assy Self for sure. The sky's the limit when we get out of our way and see what's possible when we choose to change.

Action Items:

Setting Intention:

1. Create clarity around what you want. Most of us know what we don't want clearly. Get out the paper and fold it in half. On the top of the left-hand side, label it DON'T WANT, and on the right-hand side, label it WANT. Begin by numbering all the things you don't want first! Write, and write and write, come back later and write some more, get it out! Emoting is healing!

   Now look at the 1st column, directly across from the #1 listed item,

   Look at it from the perspective of what the polar opposite is.

   This will create a better understanding of what you want.

2. Next, buy yourself a journal, a beautifully covered one that speaks to you, as well as your favorite colored pen. You are now telling your brain you are committing to YOU!

   Get yourself or make dividers; get creative! This is your journal. No one gets to see but you.

Divided into five sections:

1. Label, Gratitude,
2. Warm and Fuzzies,
3. Things I wish to accomplish (Bucket List),
4. Affirmations,
5. Quotes/ songs that speak to my Soul
6. Daily reflections (what lessons you've learned, wins, and celebrations)

1. List a minimum of 3 things you're grateful for each day. If you're in the bathroom on a roll doing it, keep on. Minimum 3 / day and caveat: You can not repeat the things for which you're grateful!

2. Warm and Fuzzies: Smile makers are things that make you smile and feel good when you think about them.

3. Your bucket list: What I want to accomplish or do with my life is 1. Be a _____ fill in the blanks. What I will be seeing or doing is _____. Get the drift?

4. Affirmations always begin with an I AM statement. IE: I am powerful, beautiful ... energetic words you wish to expand and take on within your life. Things you can and will believe about yourself, as you will be communicating to your brain this is what you want. Part of shifting the old energy.

5. There is always that one song or quote that lifts us and speaks to our soul in the moment. List them here.

6. Daily reflections: What lessons did you learn about yourself today? How might you use these lessons to grow your tomorrow? Remember, knowledge is just knowledge until it's applied!! What were your wins? Acknowledgment grows more and wins magically, especially when you choose to celebrate, no matter how big or

small; how will you celebrate? Self-reflection is key to opening up doors of self-discovery.

I always like to date each of my entries as I do; when I look back over them, I see how far I've come and how much I've grown and expanded.

Keep it up each day, and watch the magical shifts!

3. Take time for you!! Pause break. Meditate and take time in nature. Make time for fun, play, and relaxation.

4. Get yourself support where needed, we are not meant to be doing life alone. We aren't always taught tools and strategies for life challenges. That's not a bad thing, nor is it a reflection of who you are or aren't, it's not your identity. It's just what it is.

Being Classy is stepping into your authentic self, with a sassy kind of attitude that is unique to you.

Being bad-assy is being courageous and asking for support, taking action to get what you want, living the life you desire, and finding your unique definition of personal freedom.

Karen Rudolf stands as a beacon of transformation and empowerment in the realms of stress reduction and personal and professional development. As a 'Super Stress Reducer,' a 5X International Best Selling Collaborative Author, renowned speaker, podcaster, and workshop facilitator, Karen's mission is to elevate lives and nurture growth across all spheres.

Her journey is fueled by a deep-rooted passion for communication and "W" holistic well-being, guiding individuals to surmount challenges and flourish. Karen's expertise is not confined to one domain; she excels in transforming lives through innovative communication strategies, self-leadership techniques, and a foundational "W" holistic approach, marking her as a cornerstone of well-being all while creating fun and play.

Embarking on her path as a Life Strategist and Catalyst for Change, Karen's narrative is enriched by her nursing background, complemented by an extensive array of licensures and certifications. Her approach is underpinned by the 7 Pillars of Health, encapsulating a "W" holistic perspective on personal and professional evolution. This unique blend of knowledge and experience positions Karen as a multifaceted guide for those seeking to navigate the complexities of their lives. With each interaction, she aims to unlock the potential within, fostering resilience, clarity, and progress. Karen Rudolf is more than a mentor; she is a partner in the journey of transformation, dedicated to empowering each individual on their unique path toward achieving a balanced and fulfilling life.

Karen can be hired for conferences, speaking engagements, coaching, and facilitating at:

407-920-4288
www.tranquilSOULutions.com
https://www.linkedin.com/in/tranquilsoulutions/
https://www.facebook.com/karen.rudolf.14/
https://www.instagram.com/tranquilsoulutions/

Check out

Awakening Potential Podcast:
https://open.spotify.com/show/4YWLGUPg3rWtumXl084oEJ

Grab yours complimentary: 'A SOUL-opreneur's Stress Relief Checklist' at: https://www.freegiftfromkaren.com

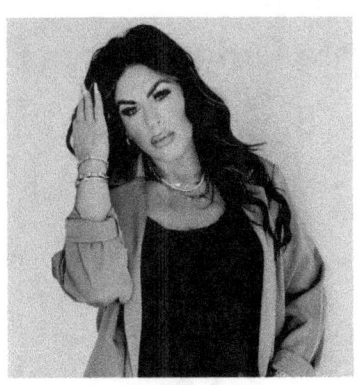

Laurie L. Graham

Boss Babe Creative LLC
Brand & Social Media Expert

https://www.facebook.com/LaurieLGraham
https://www.instagram.com/laurielgraham/
https://www.laurielgraham.com/
http://bossbabecreative.com/

I'm Laurie, your go-to natural-born hype girl, seasoned photographer, and dynamic producer. With over two decades in design, marketing, sales, business development, and coaching, my journey has been rich and rewarding. The past ten years have been dedicated to coaching home staging business owners, empowering them to build the business they love, leveraging my extensive experience in the real estate industry. I specialize in helping boss babes and small business owners catapult their ventures through strategic branding, engaging social media, and impactful content creation. My services include Instagram and Facebook content management, professional headshots, dream strategy sessions, both one-on-one and group coaching, professional videography, and staff training for those overseeing these areas. As a professional speaker, I inspire audiences to elevate their business strategies. My ultimate goal is to help you develop a brand that truly reflects your unique message, enabling you to make a lasting impact in the world.

From Corporate Girlie to Boss Babe: Keeping it Classy, Sassy, & a Little Badassy

By Laurie L. Graham

Dedication

This chapter is lovingly dedicated to the pillars of my strength and success:

To my amazing husband, Vincent, who has been my rock and steadfast supporter through every twist and turn.

To my sister Dawn, my protector, who has always stood by my side, guarding me with her unwavering strength and love.

To my son Austin, my constant reminder to "keep pushin" forward, no matter the obstacles.

To my bestie Paige, a true lifesaver whose belief in me was unshakeable even when I doubted myself.

And in honor of my momma, the strongest woman I know, Barbara Ann Hart, whose resilience and grace inspire me every day.

I am immeasurably grateful to each of you. I would not be where I am today without your love, support, and faith in me. Thank you for believing in me when I struggled to believe in myself.

Introduction: The Turning Point

Picture this: I'm deep into what feels like an endless Zoom call with the entire staff, facing an onslaught of subtle digs from the person I once revered—my boss. As she criticizes my readiness to represent our company at an upcoming event, my phone lights up with texts from colleagues cringing at her harsh words, and I just wanted to slide under my desk and disappear forever. This moment, agonizing and revealing, sparks a realization—it's time for me to take flight.

Rewind six years. I had thrown myself into my corporate role with unmatched zeal. Beyond just being a creative coordinator, I was a stylist, a confidante, and a travel companion, and I worked my way up to VP of Operations. When I tell you I was all in—I was all in. For years, I reveled in the hustle, thriving in the shadow of a powerhouse woman, absorbing every lesson about leadership and success, and until one day, it all changed.

Realization of Self-Worth

As I sat there, tears streaking down after that call, I felt a mix of betrayal, humiliation, and hurt from someone I had once admired. Can you relate? This was the push, although so painful, and it was exactly what I needed, even if I didn't know it at the time. It was time to break free from the corporate grind and create something spectacular of my own—a venture I could pour my heart into, but I lacked confidence in myself and was frozen in fear.

Growing up, I always knew I was destined to stand out. Whether it was "borrowing" my mom and sister's wardrobes or being the first on the dance floor at my parents' 80's shindigs, I shined brightly. Yet, life wasn't without its shadows. Early challenges rattled my confidence and left me feeling tarnished and unworthy.

Adversity as a Catalyst

My teenage years brought new trials: a misguided romance led to early motherhood, attracting judgment and harsh whispers. "You'll always struggle," they said. "You'll never amount to anything," they believed. As I navigated through an abusive relationship, society's labels seemed to confirm my fears—I was living down to every dismal expectation.

Silent Successes

Despite the turmoil in my personal life, I consistently thrived in my career. Each job was a stage on which I performed and excelled, climbing from entry-level positions to management roles in every post I held. Looking back, I realize that although I never envisioned myself as a business owner, I was acquiring all the experience I would need to launch my own venture. I refer to this period as my 'business boot camp' era—it taught me resilience and the art of turning chaos into opportunity. While my personal life was in disarray, professionally, I was striking gold.

Rebirth and Empowerment

After enduring several years in an abusive relationship, I was finally rescued by my family and relocated hundreds of miles away, marking the beginning of my true rebirth. This dramatic change was more than just a shift in location; it was an opportunity to rediscover who I was meant to be. As I healed, a fierce determination to empower others ignited within me, and looking back, I can see how these experiences have come full circle to shape what I do today.

I began volunteering with a youth group driven by a desire to shield young girls from the feelings of guilt, shame, and unworthiness that I knew all too well. For 15 years, I mentored teens, which eventually led me to launch my own initiative, the HUG Movement—Head Up Gorgeous. We aimed to empower women and encourage them to shine through events and Bible studies. Unfortunately, the pandemic halted our gatherings, and I redirected my focus fully to my corporate job.

The Corporate Departure

Back in the corporate world, I thrived by uplifting others and igniting their dreams. Yet, I clung to that job like a safety net, duped into believing I wasn't good enough. Despite excelling in every role I tackled, the toxic environment at work started to erode my confidence. I found myself caught in a relentless cycle of feeling swamped, undervalued, and doubting my own capabilities—struggling in roles I used to dominate. This period of self-doubt led to a crucial moment of introspection where I realized that the issue wasn't the job itself; rather, it was how deeply I had let it define me.

Therapy proved to be a game-changer for me. It peeled back the layers of my professional life, revealing a harsh reality of micromanagement, undervaluation, and a barrage of broken promises—haunting echoes of my past traumas. This revelation was a turning point. I decided to rewrite my narrative from victim to victor, investing in personal coaching that brought clarity to the drama unfolding around me. Standing up for myself became not just a choice but a necessity.

However, as the company's integrity began to wane and leadership practices shifted in a direction I couldn't ethically align with, I knew significant change was imperative. I started laying the groundwork for my own venture, Boss Babe Creative, with a focus on motivational speaking, branding, and content creation. My goal was clear: to empower other women to build businesses they love and to claim their independence just as I was preparing to claim mine.

Liberation and Launch

Reflecting on my past, I often chastise myself for not heeding my instincts sooner. My blind loyalty to someone I considered a friend cost me years filled with tears, toil, and misplaced trust. This painful experience sharpened my ability to recognize red flags and taught me the importance of acting decisively before situations deteriorate.

So, let this be your call to arms. Don't just sit around waiting for the perfect moment; seize your destiny with confidence and make magic happen. Allow my journey—my missteps and my triumphs—to inspire and empower you to "Go Boldly." Start building the business or life you dream of, even if you feel unprepared for what's to come. Often, you'll find that creating something you love is exactly what ignites your passion and fuels your soul.

Trust in your own brilliance, steer clear of unnecessary drama, and never linger in situations that sour your spirit. You are destined for a life filled with success and joy, uniquely tailored just for you.

Building the Dream

With my husband and bestie firmly in my corner, cheering me on, I began laying the foundation for my business about ten months before its official launch. Truth be told, they were the ones persistently urging me to leave, to stop tolerating such poor treatment, reminding me that I deserved so much better. Ultimately, it was a colleague who was fully aware of my situation who gave me the wake-up call I needed. She bluntly told me I was suffering from Stockholm syndrome—and she wasn't wrong. *(thank you, Michelle)*

By the time I was ready—or perhaps it's more accurate to say, compelled—to step out on my own, I had already secured several clients. Remarkably, these were enough to replace my corporate paycheck from the very first day! The unwavering support from my network of mentors, friends, and family—these incredible women who believed in and invested in my vision—was absolutely pivotal. They not only provided emotional backing but also empowered me to make that critical leap into entrepreneurship.

Leadership Redefined: A True Boss Babe

Throughout this journey, I've gained a deep understanding of what true leadership embodies. It's about being a classy, sassy, and badassy boss babe—a role that's certainly not for the faint of heart. A real boss babe uplifts others with love and honesty rather than tearing them down. They solve problems rather than create them, nurturing and elevating those around them without stepping on anyone to climb higher. True boss babes remain authentic, sticking to their principles; they are nurturers by nature, genuinely caring for others, adapting to challenges, fostering a thriving team culture, and demonstrating resilience.

These are the attributes I've woven into the fabric of my business plan for Boss Babe Creative. They reflect the lessons learned from many successful women who've been in the game longer than I have—women who embody class, sass, and badassery. These qualities are likely recognizable in you, too, even if you haven't fully realized it.

I challenge you to ask a trusted friend if they see these traits in you. If you find yourself nodding along, feeling that telltale lump in your throat, or holding back tears as you read this, then yes, this message is for you. It's a confirmation that you already possess the leadership qualities needed to transition from corporate girl to boss babe. Embrace this realization, and let it propel you forward into the business world with confidence.

Go Boldly, Boss Babe

To anyone feeling stuck or underappreciated in the corporate world but too afraid to make a move, remember: the desire to create and lead is within you. Don't wait. Move boldly towards your dreams. Surround yourself with supportive people, learn from every experience, and never doubt your worth. I firmly believe that every woman possesses an innate blend of class, sass, and badassery—it's in the journeys we take, the experiences we endure, and the challenges we overcome that this truly shines through.

Take it from me—I was once broken, used, and abused, told I would never amount to anything. Yet, here I am today, standing strong. I'm happily married to my wonderful husband of 17 years, my son and his wife enjoy successful careers and are thriving in their marriage, and I have become a bona fide boss babe committed to helping other women build the businesses they love. This transformation wasn't easy, but it was worth every step.

You can do the dang thing! Build the business you love with the support of those who believe in you. It's your time to shine.

Now, go boldly, Boss Babe, and build the business you love!

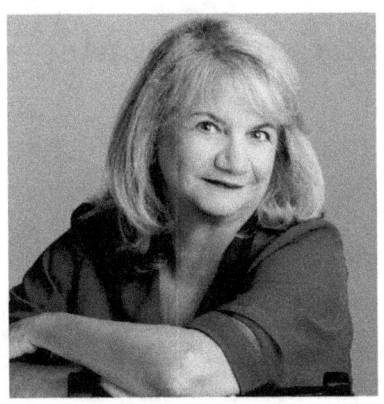

Lucia Catherine

Author

www.linkedin.com/in/lucia-catherine
https://www.facebook.com/LuciaCatherineAuthor
https://www.instagram.com/authorluciacatherine/
https://luciacatherine.com/

Lucia Catherine is an award winning internationally published author. She's a wife, mother, a grandmother and animal rescue volunteer. She creates stories about transformation, love and happiness. Her stories are sharp, honest, real, intense and sometimes have a comical edge. She resides at the beaches of Lower Delaware, where she finds most of her inspiration. Lucia loves spending time with her family and friends. She's addicted to coffee, chocolate, good books, being on the water, and her dogs.

Echoes Of Me

By Lucia Catherine

Naivety, is it part of the human spirit or a character trait? I'm still not sure I know the answer. My life changed on a rainy September Saturday, not because of tragic events but because of innocence. What are the expectations for a nineteen-year-old? I stood in the vestibule of the ancient Catholic church gripping my father's hand, trembling and knowing that any second, the doors would open, and I'd walk down the aisle to one of the biggest mistakes of my life, my father turned to me and asked, "Are you sure? We can walk right out this door and go home."

I briefly pondered his offer, but then I thought, if I did, we'd probably never see a day of peace. My fiancé, Andre, was a vindictive person. While he never behaved like that toward me, I knew what he was capable of. Then there was the fact that the entire wedding was paid for. We didn't come from money, and we lived paycheck to paycheck in a small row home in the inner city.

The ceremony was quick, and in a matter of thirty minutes, I was married. Did I love him? Looking back, I thought I did. But who knows what love is at nineteen? The rest of the day was spent cajoling him into cooperating during the festivities. The first dance as husband and wife was a hard no. I remember feeling disappointed in everything and regretted not running away when my father offered me the option.

I took a week off from work to move into his house; we didn't go on a honeymoon because he didn't want to spend the money on one. He showed his temper in week two. There was a bit of dust on top of the entertainment center. In a fit of anger, he swiped at the wedding champagne glasses that sat on top, breaking the one embossed with the word bride. Was that symbolic? Did it mean that I, too, would be broken like the shattered glass I saw in front of me? Was I overthinking? Knowing then and there, I made a mistake in marrying this man. Why did I feel I had to be the person he needed? Why wasn't he the person I needed?

My parents were happy; their love for one another was obvious to me. I learned that she took care of him, and he, in turn, took care of her. She enjoyed being a stay-at-home mom. We were her life. That's all I wanted, a marriage like theirs.

I worked in an office at a federal shipyard near our house. My home life was stressful, and so was my work life. Being the youngest, Maxine, the office manager, bullied me constantly. But I pushed through each day with respect and worked hard. Maxine left for training in another state for three months, during which the temporary manager took me under her wing and had me trained in everyone's job duties, although Maxine only used my skills for filing paperwork. My position description was not that of a filing clerk. I learned while she was gone that the other team members did the filing prior to my arrival. They each grabbed a pile before the day ended, and the bin was empty before they left for the evening. I enjoyed those three months. Once she returned and learned I knew how to do everyone's job, her toxic behavior accelerated. Back to filing only, lots of rude stare-downs and muttered remarks. I kept quiet and respectful.

The most senior team member, a quiet woman well beyond retirement age, whispered to me. "I know someone in another office. Would you like me to ask if she has any openings?" I cast my gaze on Maxine's squinted eyes and nodded. Three weeks later, I was gone and working in an accounting office where I was still the youngest but in an office managed by three supportive women. Each day, I found a reason to smile. I didn't mind at all when Delores, the division chief, referred to me as "the baby" because it was done with love. I had a sense of belonging, like being part of a family. Delores encouraged me to go to college and helped me complete the paperwork for the reimbursement program. She could tell by my facial expressions when I had a rough night at home and would call me into her office just to chat, never to be intrusive. She was just a tiny spitfire of a woman and well-respected by her peers. She was the only female division chief in the entire department. Her coffee-colored eyes and soft brown hand would hold on to mine as she talked, knowing just how to calm me without asking what was wrong. Delores died suddenly in my second year working with the team. We were all left devastated by her passing, but it hit me a little harder. The person who recognized my professional potential the most, my mentor, was gone.

My career took off after attending college. I emulated Delores' strength and kindness throughout my government career. Yet, my personal life was in shambles. Where Delores reinforced my belief in myself and my skills, my husband wore me down with name-calling, demands, and spite work. I could maintain my dignity in the office, but at home, I was a trembling semblance of the person I wanted to be.

During our thirteen-year marriage, we separated three times, once for almost a year. That last separation seemed to change him for the better. We reunited, left the city, and bought a single home in the suburbs. We decided we were ready for a baby. After much difficulty with infertility, I conceived, and that nine-month period was the best of our marriage. He was kind of fun and treated me like a princess. He wasn't the same man of the previous decade. It was an extreme nine-year marriage, but this new him I could deal with easily.

Andre's true colors resurfaced immediately after our son was born. He refused to go into the delivery room and barely visited, and the night before my release from the hospital, he came for the complimentary steak dinner in a suit. My first thought was that it was romantic, but then I remembered the kind of man he was and asked about the suit. He informed me he had a security job to do for a friend at a massive event in a local hotel. As soon as our food arrived, the baby fussed. Recovering from a C-section, I struggled to get out of bed. He ignored me and shoved food in his mouth as the baby cried. My hospital roommate told me to stay in bed and grabbed my son for me. Her expression when she peered at my son's father gave me pause. At that moment, I spiraled. He finished his food while mine got cold, tossed his napkin on his plate, and said, "Well, that sucked. I have to go." He left without a kiss, and with a quick glance at his son, he took off.

My roommate asked, "Is he always like that?" All I could do was nod. The next morning, we were to be released. Andre was late. I called him and woke him up. Woke. Him. Up. He said he worked late and told me to ask my father to come get us. This wasn't Andres' regular job. He did a favor for someone. He was supposed to bring the car seat the night before and forgot it. When the discharge nurse asked to see it, I had to call him again to ask where it was. It was still at home. I then had to call my mother, who hurried to my house and grabbed it from the porch. Meanwhile, my father wanted to take me home to their house, furious at how he treated me. At that moment, I knew my marriage was over, and I would move forward, being the best mom and person I could be.

Two months later, while on maternity leave, I received a call from HR asking when I could return. I planned to stay out until January when I learned a position was opening up in October. It was the end of the fiscal year, and the department was in a panic. When my name came up as a qualified employee, HR reached out with an offer. I agreed to become the department's budget analyst. I returned to work at the beginning of September to train with the current incumbent. He refused to train me during that month. I networked with other budget analysts. Each time he used me as a delivery girl, I took the opportunity to speak to and learn from other experienced analysts. After he left, I struggled some but persevered to learn. Three months into the job, my boss came in and looked at my empty inbox and said, "I haven't even updated my files with a deadline, and the completed work is on my desk. I must admit, I was apprehensive about you, a new mother and someone so young. But you have impressed me." It wasn't long after that our new captain called me into his office for a budget briefing, my first. I was nervous. The easel fell, and the captain laughed and apologized since he set it up. Afterward, he sent me a comic strip through interoffice mail. He wrote, "Your first briefing, my best. Well done!" Later, I received an outstanding performance rating and an award check after the Shipyard commander called our captain and told him out of all the annual budgets he received from the departments, mine was the best. Commander claimed it was professional, realistic, and achievable. He told the captain I delivered it with knowledge and could answer all of his questions. He felt the need to reach out when he learned I was the only woman budget analyst and the youngest.

My new job and the encouragement of my boss gave me the confidence I needed to grow as a career woman and a mother. While still married and living in the house I shared with my husband, I didn't consider myself a wife. I didn't need to be a better wife; he needed to do better. I spent the next year quietly preparing for single motherhood. Saving what I could and gathering sentimental things and taking them to my mom's. I knew his vindictive side and knew he would destroy anything I left behind. All the while, he built what I called a prison around me. He had the kitchen modernized, although I told him it was unnecessary, and the same was true with the bathroom. When we went shopping for a bedroom set for my two-year-old son, he found a new one for us. I stated we didn't need one, nor did I want it. He watched while I paid for our son's furniture, never once offering to pay for it. Two days later, he mentioned he returned to the furniture store and ordered the set he liked, and it would arrive with our son's set. I think he suspected something when the intimacy stopped. Andre worked shifts, and during his day shifts, we'd share a bed. I went to bed, and at the same time, I put my son to bed and was asleep before he climbed into bed.

A dear friend once advised me, "You'll know when it's time to leave. Just prepare for that moment."

It was a brisk, wintry Friday evening after Christmas when things came to a head. He was off and watching TV in the downstairs family room while my son and I watched from the bedroom. My husband came in when he came up for a snack. He sat on the corner of the bed and asked, "You're leaving me, aren't you?" Shocked, I could only nod. My son lay beside me. He then asked, "When?"

"After the holidays." Which was just days away.

"Is there anything I could do or say to make you stay?"

"Nothing. I need to do this for my mental health and to raise the baby in a calm environment." I wasn't calm. Every day after work, I vomited in the driveway, knowing I'd have to go inside, never knowing what kind of mood he'd be in.

"Well then, don't wait. Do what you have to do." The next morning, while he was at work, I loaded my car with my son's things and brought them to my parents. When he returned, he asked again what he could do to make me stay. After nine years of the same battles, shouldn't he have known?

While stomach acid was in my throat, all I said was it was too late. I needed to get away from the toxic environment. That day is still a vivid memory. I left just as the sun lowered. He followed me outside and watched as I struggled to secure my son in the car seat, his arms folded. Over the years, I secretly referred to his position as his war stance. I whispered, "I'm sorry," and slid into the driver's seat and backed out of the driveway. I almost returned when I saw him in the rearview mirror in the middle of the road, watching us leave, his arms still folded across his chest. It's odd how one position could be so triggering. I lowered my eyes and pushed toward the future.

Divorce isn't pleasant. It's the end of what you thought would be forever. Our divorce was horrible. I felt like I was anointed by fire. Everything was a battle. The constant phone calls and vandalism. He hired someone to follow me. Andre called the military police and told them I was transporting drugs onto a military installation. He tried to destroy me emotionally and professionally. After the police searched my car and my briefcase, I explained I was divorcing a police officer, and he was using his tools and power to destroy me. My co-workers, supervisor, and captain witnessed what had transpired before the military police let me go. My morning was filled with fielding calls from friends and meetings with both my boss and the captain. With their help, I received the support I needed and gained clarity on my next move. I had to leave the state. When I told Andre I had received a job offer over six hundred miles away and was going to take it, he begged me not to leave and said he would be better. He never truly admitted guilt, but I lived with the man for thirteen years and knew how he operated. When he'd get angry throughout the divorce, he'd complain that I was using our son as a weapon. Maybe I was, but it was about protecting myself so I could be an exemplary mother to him. He accused me of getting what I wanted, a baby, and of taking my toys and leaving when I got bored with him. Bored? More like an anxiety-ridden, vomiting version of myself. He told me I needed to pull my head from the sand and face normal life.

I did all that I could to get my sass back. I saw a psychologist on my doctor's recommendation. He was extremely helpful and told me it was okay to hide my head in the sand before facing problems or difficulties. It was my mind's way of preparing myself, and once I pulled my head up, I would rise like a Phoenix and conquer the problem. Maybe I stayed buried in the grains longer than I should have, but I changed and became stronger.

We tried being friends and co-parents. He asked me to iron his shirt for his first date. I did it with a grateful heart. He was moving on, and it gave me a sense of freedom. My friends thought I was ridiculous for helping him on his first date. But why wouldn't I? I had zero interest in being part of his life but didn't wish him to be lonely for the rest of his life.

Several months later, I went on a date with a coworker. We'd known each other for years but in a professional capacity. After that first date, several more followed, and I found myself in an amazingly healthy relationship. He respected me, opened doors for me, and was great with my son. Dates often included him with trips to child-friendly places. My parents adored him, too. We were secretive about our relationship since we worked together, and we worried about favoritism. I controlled the budget for the team's projects, and we thought if I approved his projects and declined others, it would be problematic.

My estranged husband often showed up unexpectedly at my parent's house, knowing my mother was home alone and our son was in preschool. He'd boldly walk into my bedroom and root through my things. He found a picture frame of me and my boyfriend and destroyed it, leaving it in the middle of my bed, the photo torn and glass broken. In order to protect my parents, I began looking for houses. I found a beautiful new community of townhomes nearby and bought my first home as a single woman. It was fun choosing my color schemes and extras without having to consider anyone else's opinion. Moreover, I wanted a safe environment to raise my son, something I could afford alone. It was important to me to be self-sufficient and not rely on anyone else. I closed on the house Labor Day weekend. How appropriate that the fruits of my job afforded this luxury townhome for me and my boy.

My son's father remarried nine months after our divorce was final. We learned shortly after that our son had significant developmental delays and subsequent diagnoses of Autism Spectrum Disorder and Pervasive Developmental Delay. During the evaluations, we also learned he had a brain tumor, which, thank God, was benign. My then-boyfriend was with me every step of the way for doctor appointments and tests; he was there to support us.

While a portion of my personal life spiraled, my career was on an upswing. My knowledge and strong work ethic earned me respect. During National Women's Week, they asked me to speak to the female employees about budgeting and finances. It was an overwhelming request for an introvert. Regardless, I felt grateful for being given this opportunity. The event took place in the installation's largest auditorium. Afterward, I opened to questions. Many of the women present were single mothers and asked how I navigated it. I explained honestly, sometimes with humor, and held nothing back. I ended with, "We are not the weaker sex; we are superhumans that can do anything we set our minds and hearts to." A few days later, the shipyard commander sent me a thank-you note. In his note, he wrote my speech was intelligent and informative and had him laughing out loud while being a class act. I was unaware he was listening by the door.

By that August, I was engaged and planned to be married in April. I wish I could say things were easier with my former husband that first year, but they weren't. Although he'd remarried, he tried to keep his finger on the pulse of my life. I didn't tell him I was getting married because he threatened that my new husband wouldn't make it out of the ceremony alive. We kept everything secret and encouraged the invitees not to tell anyone, not even my son. Despite the lingering threat, the wedding was wonderful, as was the honeymoon.

The week after our dream honeymoon, Andre picked up my son on a Saturday morning, earlier than scheduled. I answered the door, thinking it was a neighbor. I didn't invite him inside because I recognized the expression on his face. Evil. Vindictive. I requested he wait in his car as I assisted my son with his shoes. Calling from the opened door, he labeled my husband a coward for hiding in the bedroom. He was not. He was still asleep. John heard the rude remark but didn't respond. I had begged him frequently not to engage with him, and I was grateful he had taken the advice.

My marriage was everything I dreamed of. John was a loving and supportive husband and doting stepfather. He demanded nothing and never told me to ask for permission. I was an equal partner, and we shared everything.

Andre was still combative. My mother decided it was best for us to bring my son to them, and they would do the handoff, or I would do it with them present. Andre asked why I refused to do it myself. After explaining that his behavior was abhorrent and that I refused to be subjected to it, he changed. Andre became a better man and father. He was then welcome to come to our house to pick up our son.

In late 1993, we were told the Shipyard was part of the Base Realignment and Closure. Both John and I were losing our jobs. We were building a large home in which to raise a family. We learned shortly thereafter that we would be placed on a Priority Placement list, meaning we would get jobs before hiring from the outside. The problem for us was that we both worked for the same installation, and we were being offered a geographic region rather than the city in which we worked. If you refused a position, they removed you from the program. There were many reasons I couldn't leave the Philadelphia area. One was my son's health issues. The Children's Hospital of Philadelphia was excellent with his many issues, and we appreciated the care he received. Then there was the divorce decree, which stated I could only live within thirty miles of the area where we lived when our son was born. This was winnable in court, did I really want to fight it, knowing the battle it would start? Also, both of our families lived nearby.

It was during this time that my dad retired on disability for a bone disease, and it was getting challenging for him to navigate steps. My parents wanted to move to their smaller, one-level summer house on the Jersey shore. Much too far to be my son's caregiver. John had a plan in mind and worried about how to approach it with me, so first, he talked to my father since I provided the larger income in our household. All my father said was, "Good luck. My daughter doesn't like domesticity; she is a career woman." Eventually, John knocked on my office door at work. We kept it professional at work, and he rarely came into my office unless it was lunchtime, and, for propriety's sake, we always kept the door open. We worked with a lot of fun but raunchy teammates who would love to rib us. He closed the door, and I remember being surprised. He pulled a chair to my desk and proposed that I become a stay-at-home mom. We were still learning the depths of Michael's issues, and there would still be a lot of medical appointments. My current boss understood, perhaps a new one wouldn't. He also told me he'd received a job offer that morning and could start in a few weeks. The downside of my being home was we had to get out of the deal with the new house and either stay in the townhouse or buy something less expensive.

We found a lovely home in an established, beautiful, tree-lined neighborhood. Everything fell into place. We sold the townhouse, and I learned we were having our first baby together; I agreed that being a stay-at-home mom made sense.

During my second pregnancy, John and I experienced our first tragedy as a married couple. Our baby died in utero at almost sixteen weeks. Two days later, while I was recovering at home, Andre delivered our son to me. He had sent him home with chocolates and a bouquet.

The years flew by, and my former husband mellowed and became a friend. When our two youngest sons were born, he never forgot a birthday or holiday.

When the doctor diagnosed Andre with a brain tumor, I volunteered to help his wife. I took her to the hospital each day and planned to be the one to take Andre to Philadelphia for his treatment because she had a severely ill mother at home whom she was caring for. The staff nicknamed us "sister wives" because of our unique relationship. Andre passed away two months after the diagnosis. His wife invited me to the funeral home to help plan his service. Although honored, I mentioned it wasn't necessary, and it wasn't my place. His wife insisted. She confided during their marriage that he admitted to everything that went wrong in ours, and he took ownership. She told me that knowing what he did to me, for me to step up and help, showed my strength and forgiveness. When things had taken a turn for the worse, I asked her for a moment alone with him. I took his hand and prayed over him. I expressed regret for my part in the marriage's dissolution and forgave him for his. Despite the sedation, Andre squeezed my hand, indicating he heard me.

It's funny how a person perceives themselves. I never thought of myself as strong. I push along, getting things done and helping others whenever I can. My sister-in-law says I am the strongest person she knows. Probably not, but I'm determined. I'm a work in progress and will continue to be. I'm confident in my ability to bring sass, even the badassy moments. It's challenging to be classy all the time because the other two are so much more fun.

If I can offer the readers any advice, it would be that relationships, along with intimacy, are all about giving and taking. It's okay to give, but be sure to take it too. You can be in control of what makes you happy. Be unashamed of your needs and desires, both inside and outside the bedroom. In today's climate, you'd think women wouldn't still be on the back burner. Yet, at times, we are. While society may be broken, don't let it break you.

After many life changes, I'm enjoying retirement with my husband of thirty-one years. Yes, I returned to the workforce when my boys were old enough to go to school full-time. I scored an amazing work-at-home job as a Marketing Manager for a marketing agency. Our three sons are grown, and we recently welcomed our first grandchild, a precious baby girl. Life isn't always easy, especially after a diagnosis of early-stage breast cancer. While the diagnosis set me back a beat or two emotionally, I'm a survivor and plan to enjoy my life to its fullest.

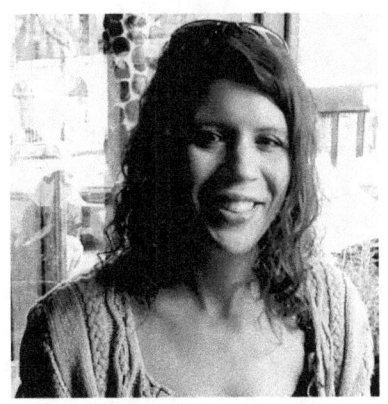

Mercedes Aspland

CEO of ITA Community

https://www.facebook.com/groups/spiritualempoweredwomen
https://www.instagram.com/mercedesaspland
https://itacommunity.com
https://www.groweatmove.com

Mercedes is a transformation coach and course creator. She uses her own unique method called Luminous Life Method. This helps her clients make big shifts in their businesses, mindset, and lives. She works with chakras, energy bodies, combining them with Buddhist philosophies and Ho'oponopono. Mercedes helps people understand themselves better and make more supportive decisions. She started her working life in banking but changed paths after her father's suicide. Mercedes often talks about how this tragic event affected her. Mercedes sees this event as the best thing that happened in her life. Mercedes loves helping people find their purpose and live meaningful lives.

Bold Moves:
Living Outside the Comfort Zone

By Mercedes Aspland

Introduction

What does it mean to live a badass life? That was probably the first question I asked myself when I decided to write this chapter. Could I really say anything in my life was badass? Then it hit me: the motto I live by is probably one of the most badass things you can do. "You only regret the things you don't do, not the things you do."

Sounds pretty straightforward, right? Actually, it leads you down all sorts of unusual paths when you jump into things others would shy away from. This approach has led to amazing career changes, wonderful places to live, and meetings with some of the most incredible people, adding a lot of excitement to my life.

In this chapter, I will tell you about one of the first properties I bought, about leaving a secure six-figure job and making several moves around the country. Hold on to your hats because it has been a wild ride.

Once I've gone through the ways I've jumped in and the lessons I've learned, I will share some tips on how you can live a life that's a bit more badass. You'll learn how to move out of the mundane and run-of-the-mill into a life full of excitement. This is not for you if you like a sure bet or if you need to know how things will turn out. But if you love a bit of adventure or want to start taking more risks in life, then read on.

Buying My Flat

This was one of the craziest things I have ever done. I had just agreed to buy a house with my mum with a huge mortgage, but then another opportunity arose. This was to purchase a flat in the old Arsenal stadium, something I had dreamed of from the moment they announced they were going to convert it into flats.

This meant buying a flat off-plan and having to complete the purchase about 3-4 years later. I had just started working in banking and had been given a permanent contract three weeks prior.

At the time I went to look at the flats and choose one, I had just about enough money to put down the 5% I needed to pay that day. I knew I needed to pay another 5% in three months' time, and I had no idea if I would have that money or not. But being me, I said yes and signed the contract.

Looking back, it was mad, and I'm not really sure what possessed me to do it, but there you go. Well, three months rolled around, and I received a bigger bonus than I expected, which allowed me to pay the next 5%.

What happened next was a bit harder to deal with, but by the time I needed to pay for my flat, I was no longer in banking, and the bottom had fallen out of the property market. The mortgage company said it was worth less than the price I agreed to all those years ago.

This was a scary moment in my life and one that really had me doubting my sanity. Why had I even agreed to buy this flat in the first place? With a house already, I obviously wasn't going to be able to afford to move into the property, but buying to let was a possibility. I decided to go for it, after all, I didn't have much of an option now.

I did it. I secured the property and got a tenant there. It was amazing that I managed it; it took some serious nerve to get through that time. I need to add that it left me with a lot of credit card debt that I needed to gradually pay off.

Fast forward another five years, I had managed to hold onto that property, and at that point, I decided that selling it was the best option, largely because the price had risen so much that my rental yield was pretty low. The profit I made on this property enabled me to fund a property development business later on and allowed me to build a portfolio so that I could live with relative freedom in life.

So you are probably asking yourself now, what can I get out of this story? Well, it is the fact that I jumped, had faith, and trusted that things would work out for the best. It led to some excitement and drama in my life and ended up being the single best investment I have ever made.

When I walked through the doors to look at the flats, it was the pipe dream of my teenage self, and even at 23, when I was signing the contract, it still felt like playing a game. That is something I want you to incorporate into your mindset. Life is not meant to be taken too seriously, and when you need all the answers, you reduce the chance of that big reward.

Taking a leap on this occasion took me a long way towards financial freedom and changed the course of my life forever. If you had asked me at the time, I never would have foreseen that, but if I had not taken the plunge, my life might have been a lot more of a struggle.

Leaving Banking

This story is another one about taking a leap of faith, but it arose from a different place—not from excitement, but from a deep need to love and care for myself more. Let me take you back to my childhood to explain.

Growing up, my dad was an abusive alcoholic, and I was constantly surrounded by drama and turmoil. This shaped me into a person who always wanted to please others, and doing the right thing was crucial. It led me to university and a career in banking, sidelining my creative side and the things that truly inspired me.

From the very first day I walked through the door of the bank, I hated my job. I tried to find joy in it, but it only made me ill. I celebrated every Wednesday afternoon because it meant there was less of the week left than what had already passed. By my early 30s, I regularly calculated how long I would need to stay in this job before I could afford to leave it.

Then, when I was 25, my dad committed suicide. I hadn't seen him for a few years, and it rocked my world. It was surreal because he had never really been there for me, and years of therapy helped me understand that it wasn't just him I had lost but my hope.

In the cutthroat world of banking, my boss asked me not to take any time off as the team needed me. It was then I realized my days were numbered in a job I detested, but I stuck it out a few more months.

This period in my life showed me how short time really is—you never know what's coming or how long you truly have. My family had a small web design business and offered me a position. I would be going from a six-figure salary to a much lower one, but my peace of mind was so much more valuable.

At that time, some of the more senior bankers told me I was brave to make such a move. I didn't see it as bravery but as a blessed relief from a life I absolutely detested. Looking back, it would have been so easy to stay, collect my paycheck, and be financially secure. After all, isn't that what life is about?

The truth is quite the opposite. Now, don't get me wrong, money is important, but I decided that I also wanted good physical and mental health, which I lacked at the time.

My message to you from this chapter of my life is to trust in your abilities. I knew I would be alright leaving my job. I knew I would find a way and just let things be. Success isn't about forcing yourself to do something you hate to achieve a goal; it's about finding what lights you up and using that to create your dream life.

So, if you ever find yourself feeling trapped in a life you do not want to live and perhaps never chose in the first place, consider making a change. Take a leap into the unknown and trust that the universe has your back.

The Big Move

After working in the family web design business and running an e-commerce business for a while (that is another very long story), I made another big decision. This one was to completely relocate from London to Devon.

This one was more on a whim or maybe a boost of inspiration. I decided it would be a good idea to move to the Devon/Cornwall area and went to stay there for 2 weeks. At that time, I looked all around for somewhere to live and found this great place with a swimming pool. The only catch, the owners wanted the tenancy to start in 10 days.

The crazy in me decided it was a good idea, so I went back to London, packed up, and moved to Devon in just ten days. It could have been stressful, but it was actually one of the most fun things I have ever done.

It was definitely a good move; the village I was living in was a bit remote, but I got to meet some of the locals. And how lucky I was to meet some of the most amazing people I have ever met. We had pool parties and even watched fireworks from the roof of where I was staying. More than that, though, these people have become lifelong friends.

One of the most amazing things about this time of my life was I got to learn who I really was. I had the space to meditate, chant, do yoga, and read spiritual texts. It was like a personal retreat; one where I set the rules and got to go as deep as I needed to. After years of being on the go, suffering trauma and loss it was definitely needed.

I only stayed in Devon for a year, so it was not a permanent move, but it was a defining one, and I don't regret it. It showed me the power of stepping outside of my comfort zone and finding a different way of looking at things. The joys in life can come from some of the most amazing places.

Actionable Steps to Live a More Exciting Life

I wanted to put together some tips and advice for you so that you can live a life filled with excitement. Actually having the courage to jump in and do something outside your comfort zone is terrifying at first. Finding ways to prepare for that is what is really going to make the difference to you.

Identify Your Comfort Zone Boundaries

The first thing you want to know is where you are comfortable. This might seem obvious to you, but sometimes, we are not even sure where our comfort zone is, so we don't even know if we are in or out.

This can be as simple as taking some time to reflect on the areas where you feel comfortable and areas that intimidate you. A great way to do this is to get a large piece of paper and put a circle in the middle. Inside the circle, write down all the things you enjoy, and that feel easy to you. You might include work tasks that you find a breeze, places you go to regularly, people you are your true self with, etc.

Now on the outside of this circle, list activities, career moves, or social interactions that you avoid. Think of places that you rarely travel to or things that make you feel uncomfortable. For example, someone I know hates to travel by train, so that would be outside the circle.

It is important when you do this task that you are honest with yourself, we are all guilty of glossing over negative emotions but this is not the time. Unless you are 100% comfortable with it, it goes outside the circle.

So now you know all the things that are outside your comfort zone, all the things that make your heart beat a bit faster. Maybe you can include things you would like to do in this area but have never had the courage to do.

I am a big believer in visualization and so now you have this diagram you can use it for a visualization.

> "*Take a moment to sit where you will not be disturbed and close your eyes. Take a couple of deep breaths to center yourself and imagine yourself in the middle of your circle, in your comfort zone. Look around you; see all the things that you see, what you hear, what you can feel, smell, and taste. Really take everything in. As you walk around this circle, notice how you hold yourself and how others treat you. Now you see your circle and feel the anxiety and excitement that wells up inside. Walk up to the circle and see all the amazing things on the other side. Take a deep breath and cross over; you are now outside your comfort zone. Take in all the wonderful things there for you, allow yourself to enjoy them, experience them, and know they are for you. As you spend time here, you notice your circle expanding so that all these new things are now inside your comfort zone. Stay here for as long as you are comfortable, and then when you are ready, return to the here and now while keeping that sense that your comfort zone has now expanded.*"

This is a visualization you can return to whenever you want to bring something within your comfort zone. The brain does not know the difference between doing something or visualizing doing something, so if you want to get comfortable doing something, visualize doing it first.

Set Small, Achievable Challenges

Another tactic to employ to step outside your comfort zone is to start small. Sounds simple, but this is where so many people self-sabotage. Maybe there is something you want to achieve, like public speaking. If you are terrified of public speaking, then booking yourself at an event where thousands of people are watching could be a disaster. In fact, it probably will. The truth is you have subconsciously set the bar too high so that you will fail and prove yourself right that you are too scared to speak in public.

So what could you have done instead? Maybe begin by speaking in front of 2 or 3 friends and see how that goes. If it works, then put yourself in for an event that will have maybe 10-15 people there. Build your confidence that way. After a certain amount of practice, you can tackle that huge event. Although, remember you will still have nerves you have the experience to overcome them.

These principles apply to anything you want to do. Yes, there are times when you can jump in and take a risk. I do things like that all the time but I have built up a tolerance to taking risks. If taking any kind of risk paralyzes you with fear then start small and build up your risk-taking skills. Remember too that the fear you feel is your brain's way of keeping you safe, be grateful for it and know it might just save your life one day.

Deal with Your Fear of Failure

This is such an important part of stepping outside your comfort zone. The reason most people don't is that they are afraid of failing. The "what ifs?" come out all over the place. I get that; I am guilty of feeling that on a regular basis, but there are ways to deal with it.

At times, when I need to deal with my fear of failure, I come back to a lesson I learned from Dale Carnegie. Now, as a teenager and beyond, I have read this book a lot. There is one section in it where you need to figure out what the worst thing that can happen is.

This is actually a very freeing exercise because our brain actually stops thinking when we are trying to step outside our comfort zone. We think something terrible could happen, and we don't want to think about it. When we decide on the worst-case scenario, we have something to work from because the next part is the most vital.

Once you know the worst thing that can happen, what can you do to improve on it? So for me, when leaving banking, the worst thing is I could have not had any money, ok not great. But I knew my solution was I could get another job, simple. Then suddenly the fear of not making it on my own was less scary.

When you have a solution to your problem, your brain will stop running the situation on repeat, and you can calm the nervous system. This makes it much easier to take that leap of faith.

The other thing that you can do with failure is remove the concept from your life. You might try something that might not work out the way you want. Does that mean you failed or that you learned something? The famous story goes that Edison discovered a lightbulb that worked after 999 previous attempts. He did not see any one of them as a failure, just that he had found a way that didn't work.

I would also like to add my own thoughts on this: Edison would only have been a failure if he had given up or if he had not tried in the first place. So often, our fear of failure keeps us stuck, but that inaction is a failure in itself. If you can start to see that not trying, not giving it a go, is the ultimate failure, then you will change the way you approach risk.

Think about how you will feel at the end of your life. Do you want to look back on a life of fun and experiment and potentially great wins, or do you want to have a load of coulda, shoulda wouldas to ponder?

Maintain Momentum and Build Resilience

Now, you have decided to be someone who steps outside their comfort zone and does difficult things. How do you prevent yourself from shrinking back again? How do you keep that expansive mindset?

Well, there are some everyday practices you can weave into your life to keep the momentum going. The first thing is to begin to celebrate your small wins. Every time you do something that makes you a bit scared, celebrate it, even if it is just saying hi to a new colleague or going to a new coffee shop.

So often, we miss the little things and don't realize the progress we are making. By noticing these steps and celebrating them, you reinforce your successes. Your brain will naturally look for more ways to be bold and brave, and the reward pathway will be set.

At the same time, you also want to develop coping strategies to help you deal with the fear and keep going. This can be anything that calms you and brings you back to centre. So perhaps you meditate on a regular basis and change the way your brain works.

You could also do something physical when you feel stress building, as this will help the feel-good hormones come rushing in. For me, getting out in the garden and putting my hands in the soil, which has been proven to raise my mood, helps a lot.

A deep breathing exercise can do a lot to calm you. When we are nervous and begin to panic, we breathe in and forget to exhale. So breathing in for four and exhaling for a count of 8, nice and slow can really help to calm the nervous system. This is a great one to use at a stressful moment, like before going on stage.

Once you have developed your own celebrations and coping strategies, you will find that the risk-taking is more manageable and your life flows with ease.

Constantly Reevaluate and Adjust

It is vital to keep an eye on what is happening with your comfort zone because we can quickly plateau. Regularly do the exercise from the beginning of this chapter and figure out where your comfort zone is.

The best thing about this is that you can keep a record and see all the extra things you have added to your comfort zone and keep moving yourself out of it.

Before you ask, yes, I think you should keep challenging your comfort zone for one big reason. As humans, we need a purpose and something to strive for. When you live within your comfort zone, you will turn to other things for fulfillment. That is when people get into drugs, gambling, and obsessive social media or similar pursuits.

We do these things to give us a high; it gives us a moment of fulfillment, but it does not last, so we chase the next high. Stepping outside your comfort zone takes you there. You get a buzz each time you achieve a new thing, and that pushes you on. Your life is fulfilled and overflowing with meaning; that is why I am always looking for a way to grow and push through my limits.

Always be Learning

I am definitely what could be termed a lifelong learner, whether in personal development or just learning a new skill. Maybe that is why I think it is so important, or maybe it is because it keeps you moving forward.

I mentioned in the last section how we all need a purpose and something to strive for. When we are learning it is giving us a goal to aim for and giving us more meaning. Plus, it has the added advantage of pushing us into new areas.

I can give you a perfect example of this. I always hated gardening and would try to hide when my mum said it was time to weed the garden. The things I hated the most were bugs and getting my hands dirty. Dirt under my nails made me shiver.

Then, in 2017, I moved somewhere with a big garden and thought it would be nice to have my own vegetable patch. I started this project and got hooked; I read books on gardening and watched programs and then went on a three-year learning journey to get an advanced diploma in the principles and practices of horticulture. I had no real plan for this, but it gave me meaning.

I now have an allotment, always have dirty nails, and have even found my peace with spiders. I have grown as a person, and my comfort zone is in a whole new place today. If I had not been willing to learn, I would have remained stuck and missed out on a whole area of my life that I actually love.

So my advice to anyone is to follow your desires, the things that excite you. You never know where they will lead you and what joys they will bring into your life.

In Summary

If you have followed the steps in this section then you should have a fairly good idea of where your comfort zone is and have some strategies for moving beyond it. My challenge to you is to do something today that will take you outside your comfort zone. What can you do that will shake things up, even if it is just taking a different route to work to do it? Then if you feel called to, get in touch with me and let me know how it felt.

Conclusion

Thank you for taking the time to read this chapter. When I started, I was not really sure where I was going to go with it but loved the whole process. It was quite a fitting topic really as I was definitely outside my comfort zone writing this and hope that I have given you the value I wanted to.

If I have achieved my goals, then you will understand the buzz and excitement of jumping into the unknown and just going for it. You will also have a whole host of strategies to begin taking a few more risks, and who knows, one day, you could be writing a chapter about all the badass things you have done.

To finish, I wanted to remind you of the motto by which I live my life. I am happy for you to steal it, use it, and make it part of your life. "*You won't regret the things you do, only the things you don't do.*" So next time you are deciding whether to take a leap of faith, remember these words and go for them.

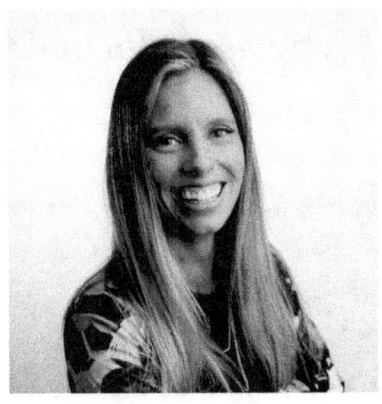

Nicole Curtis

She Rises Studios
Intl. Bestselling Author, Speaker, Crazy Chicken Lady

https://www.linkedin.com/in/nicole-curtis-sherisesstudios
https://www.facebook.com/nicolecurtiscrazychickenlady
https://www.instagram.com/nicolecurtiscrazychickenlady
https://www.sherisesstudios.com
https://www.facebook.com/groups/sherisesstudioscommunity

Nicole Curtis, an International Bestselling Author, Speaker, and self-proclaimed Crazy Chicken Lady, is a revered figure in women's leadership. With over 17 years of experience in personal growth and self-leadership development, Nicole is a sought-after expert who exudes a unique blend of personality and empowerment.

Nicole's mission is to empower women to embrace growth, elevate their lives, and expand their horizons in both personal and professional aspects. Through her engaging writing and compelling speeches, she resonates with women worldwide, encouraging them to unlock their natural leadership potential and navigate life and business authentically. With her guidance, women are inspired to step into their true selves, leading with confidence and purpose on their journey towards self-discovery and success.

Rise, Shine and Cluckin' Grind

By Nicole Curtis

In the depths of despair, I found the strength to rise. It was a journey marked by pain, resilience, and the unyielding determination to reclaim my life. From the darkest moments emerged a newfound sense of purpose—a light of hope guiding me through the storm. Each trial I faced became a stepping stone toward a brighter tomorrow, fueling my resolve to overcome adversity and emerge stronger than ever before.

Hello, I'm Nicole Curtis, aka the Crazy Chicken Lady. I am not only a survivor, entrepreneur, and advocate for inner power but also a firm believer in the transformative power of resilience. Born into a world of adversity, I've encountered challenges that tested my spirit and resolve. However, through perseverance and unwavering determination, I've emerged triumphant, refusing to let circumstances define my destiny.

Growing up in an uneasy environment, I learned early on the true meaning of resilience. From navigating the shadows of childhood trauma to facing the daunting complexities of adulthood, my journey has been anything but easy. Yet, with each obstacle encountered, I discovered a well of inner strength waiting to be unleashed. Despite the odds stacked against me, I refused to give in to despair, choosing instead to rise above adversity and embrace the fullness of life's possibilities.

In this chapter, I invite you to uncover the key themes of resilience, determination, and embracing one's inner badass. Through my story, I aim to inspire you to find comfort in your own strength, to persevere in the face of adversity, and to embrace authenticity with unwavering courage. It's a journey of self-discovery, empowerment, and unyielding resilience—a testament to the unstoppable human spirit and its capacity for growth and transformation.

Join me as I set forth on a journey through the peaks and valleys of my life, sharing the invaluable lessons learned and the triumphs achieved along the way. From overcoming childhood trauma to forging a path of entrepreneurship and empowerment, this is a tale of resilience, determination, and the unwavering pursuit of one's dreams. Through moments of vulnerability and triumph, I extend an invitation to you to join me as we explore the depths of the human experience and discover the extraordinary power within ourselves.

Theme One: Resilience (Sassy)

In the face of adversity, I've learned that resilience is not just about bouncing back but about rising stronger than ever before. It's about facing challenges head-on and refusing to let them define us.

Throughout my life, I have encountered challenges that tested my resilience. From surviving child sexual abuse to navigating the betrayal of spousal infidelity, each obstacle seemed insurmountable. The pain and betrayal cut deep, shaking the very foundation of my being. Maya Angelou once said, "You may encounter many defeats, but you must not be defeated." This quote resonates deeply with me, as it encapsulates the essence of resilience and the unwavering determination to persevere despite setbacks.

It was in these darkest challenges, that I turned to my faith for strength and guidance. I leaned on the support of friends and family, finding solace in their love and encouragement. Through prayer and reflection, I found the courage to confront my demons and emerge stronger on the other side. As I reflect on my journey of resilience, I am reminded of the incredible strength that resides within each of us. No matter what obstacles we face, we have the power to rise above adversity and rewrite our stories. Remember, resilience is not a trait we are born with—it's a skill that can be cultivated through courage, perseverance, and self-belief. So, as you navigate life's ups and downs, I urge you to embrace your inner strength and never lose sight of the limitless potential within you.

Amidst all the hurt, I began on a journey of self-discovery. Through introspection and self-love, I came to find my inner strength, which I never knew existed so strongly within me. Each setback became an opportunity for growth, and each challenge fueled my determination to reclaim my power. It was a process of shedding old wounds and embracing the truth of who I am. One poignant example of resilience in my life was the decision to seek therapy to address the trauma of child sexual abuse. Despite the stigma and shame associated with seeking help, I knew that healing was essential for my well-being. Through therapy, I learned to confront my past traumas with courage and compassion, paving the way for healing and self-acceptance.

For instance, when confronted with the trauma of child sexual abuse, I refused to let it define me. Instead, I sought therapy and support groups, finding healing through vulnerability and self-compassion. Similarly, when faced with spousal infidelity, I chose forgiveness over bitterness and resentment. It wasn't easy, but through forgiveness, I found liberation and peace.

Through moments of vulnerability and triumph, I've learned that resilience is not just about surviving—it's about thriving in the face of adversity. My journey of resilience has taught me that no matter how difficult the circumstances, there is always hope. By embracing our inner strength and leaning on the support of others who have our best interests at heart, we can overcome any obstacle that comes our way.

Theme Two- Determination (Classy)

Throughout my journey, I've always set ambitious goals for myself, driven by a relentless desire to challenge the status quo and reach new heights. In my corporate career, I set my sights on climbing the corporate ladder, determined to achieve success and make a meaningful impact in the industry. From the early days of my career, I envisioned myself in leadership positions, driving change and inspiring others through my leadership and my vision. The prospect of making a tangible difference in the corporate world fueled my ambition and propelled me forward.

As a woman in a male-dominated field, I faced unique challenges and obstacles that demanded resilience and determination. Despite the systemic barriers and biases I encountered, I refused to be limited by societal expectations or traditional gender roles. Instead, I forged ahead with confidence, determined to carve out my own path and redefine what success looked like in my industry. It wasn't easy; there were moments of doubt and frustration, but each challenge only strengthened my resolve.

Additionally, as an aspiring entrepreneur, I embarked on the daunting journey of starting my own business. Fueled by a passion for innovation and a vision for creating something truly impactful and inspirational, I took the leap into entrepreneurship with unwavering determination. The prospect of building something from scratch, of creating a legacy that would endure beyond my lifetime, ignited a fire within me and propelled me forward. Every setback was a lesson, and every obstacle was an opportunity for growth.

I sought the freedom that entrepreneurship offers—not only the freedom to be oneself and pursue one's passions but also the freedom to serve as an example to other women navigating the corporate world. I aimed to inspire and empower women who, like me, faced struggles in a predominantly male-driven corporate environment, showing them that they, too, could break barriers and achieve their dreams. It was about more than just building a successful business; it was about paving the way for future generations of women leaders.

The path to success was far from easy. In the corporate world, I faced numerous challenges, including being undervalued and underestimated by colleagues and superiors. Despite pouring my heart and soul into my work, I often found myself overlooked for promotions and opportunities. The glass ceiling seemed impenetrable, and the pervasive culture of hierarchy and favoritism presented formidable barriers to my advancement. Similarly, as I ventured into entrepreneurship, I encountered the inevitable hurdles and setbacks that come with building a business from the ground up.

From lack of funds and knowing how to navigate day-to-day operations, every day seemed to present a new obstacle to overcome. The weight of responsibility felt overwhelming at times, and the fear of failure loomed large on the horizon. Yet, in the face of adversity, I refused to fall into the trap of self-doubt or despair. Instead, I channeled my frustrations into fuel for my determination, using each setback as a stepping stone toward my ultimate goals.

Yet, through it all, my determination remained unwavering. Empower yourself by actively seeking information and knowledge, recognizing that learning is a powerful tool. Don't hesitate to seek assistance when needed, and find a supportive community where you can both learn and grow, drawing inspiration and empowerment from others. I refused to let setbacks define me or derail my ambitions. Instead, I embraced each challenge as an opportunity to grow stronger and more resilient. With every obstacle overcome, I emerged more determined than ever to achieve my goals and prove the naysayers wrong.

My journey is a testament to the power of determination and perseverance in the face of adversity. It's a reminder that success is not just about talent or luck but about resilience and unwavering commitment to one's goals. In the end, it's not the challenges we face that define us, but how we choose to respond to them. For me, the choice was clear: to rise above, to persevere, and to never lose sight of the dreams that fuel my passion and drive.

Theme Two- Embrace (Badassy)

Authenticity isn't just about being true to yourself; it's about embracing every part of your identity, even the ones that society may deem unconventional or non-conforming. There have been numerous instances in my life where I've had to stand up for what I believe in and speak my truth, even when it wasn't the popular opinion. Whether it was advocating for others, challenging outdated beliefs, or simply expressing my thoughts and feelings authentically, I've always strived to lead with integrity and stay true to my values.

One significant moment where I embraced my authenticity was during a corporate meeting where I challenged management on the prevailing opinion of operations within the sales team. Despite facing opposition and skepticism from my colleagues, I stood firm in my beliefs and articulated my perspective with conviction and clarity. While it was a risky move, I knew that staying true to my principles was more important than seeking approval or conformity. This experience taught me the importance of speaking up for what I believe in, even when it means standing alone.

From an early age, I've been a non-conformist, unafraid to challenge societal norms and expectations that didn't align with my values or beliefs. I've never been one to shy away from disrupting the status quo. By asserting my true self and living life on my own terms, I've been able to carve out a path that's uniquely mine, free from the constraints of societal expectations and limitations.

Growing up, I always felt the pressure to conform to traditional expectations. However, I refused to let society dictate who I should be as a woman or how I should live my life. Instead, I challenged these norms by pursuing my passions and interests, regardless of whether they aligned with societal expectations. I've always strived to live authentically and unapologetically.

Being badassy isn't just about being bold and brassy; it's about having the courage to show up authentically, even when it's not an easy choice. In both my personal and professional life, I've never been one to play it safe or conform to others' expectations. Instead, I've embraced my boldness and brassy nature, using it as a source of strength and empowerment. Whether it's speaking up in meetings, taking calculated risks in business, or simply being unapologetically myself, I've always approached life with a fearless attitude and a willingness to embrace my authenticity.

Both personally and professionally, I've never been one to shy away from taking risks or speaking my mind. As an entrepreneur, I've had to make bold decisions and navigate uncertain terrain, often facing criticism and doubt along the way. However, I've never let fear or insecurity hold me back from pursuing my dreams and standing up for what I believe in. I approach life with a fearless attitude and a commitment to authenticity.

I am an advocate for women to own their power and speak their truth. Never be afraid to let their voices be heard. It matters; they are worthy of it.

Reflecting on my journey, there are several key lessons and insights that have profoundly influenced my personal and professional growth. Firstly, resilience has been a cornerstone of my success. The ability to bounce back from setbacks, adapt to changing circumstances, and to persevere in the face of adversity has been instrumental in overcoming challenges and achieving my goals. Each obstacle I encountered served as an opportunity for growth, teaching me valuable lessons about resilience and determination.

Additionally, embracing my inner badass has been transformative. By boldly asserting my authenticity, challenging societal norms, and refusing to conform to others' expectations, I've been able to craft a path that's uniquely mine. This journey of self-discovery has empowered me to embrace my strengths, acknowledge my worth, and pursue my passions unapologetically. It's a reminder that true empowerment comes from within, from owning our power and embracing our uniqueness.

Practical Advice and Encouragement:

For those who may be facing similar challenges or have started on their own empowerment journey, I offer the following words of advice and encouragement:

1. **Believe in Yourself:** Self-love and self-belief are foundational to success. Trust in your abilities, celebrate your achievements, and embrace your worthiness. Remember, you are capable of achieving greatness.

2. **Embrace Failure as Growth:** Failure is not a reflection of your worth; it's an opportunity for growth. Embrace setbacks as learning experiences, and use them to fuel your determination and resilience. Remember, every successful person has faced adversity along the way.

3. **Stay True to Your Authenticity:** Don't be afraid to be yourself, even if it means standing out from the crowd. Your authenticity is your greatest asset, and it's what sets you apart from others. Embrace your uniqueness, and let your true self shine.

4. **Surround Yourself with Support:** Seek out mentors, allies, and a supportive community that uplifts and empowers you. Surrounding yourself with positive influences can provide encouragement, guidance, and perspective during challenging times.

5. **Keep Moving Forward:** No matter how daunting the journey may seem, keep moving forward with courage and determination.

Break your goals down into manageable steps, and celebrate your progress along the way. Remember, every step forward brings you closer to your dreams.

6. **Find Your Power:** To truly find your power, you must go on a journey of self-discovery that dives into the depths of your being (mind, body, and soul). Begin by reflecting on your experiences, values, and aspirations. Take the time to understand what drives you, what holds you back, and what you truly want out of life. Cultivate self-awareness by paying attention to your thoughts, emotions, and behaviors, allowing you to make choices that are authentic and aligned with your true self. Remember to be gentle with yourself and practice self-forgiveness, letting go of past mistakes and embracing the lessons they taught you. By embracing self-reflection, self-awareness, and self-forgiveness, you'll unlock the power within you and find the courage to live life on your own terms.

My journey has been a testament to the indomitable human spirit and the power of resilience, determination, and embracing one's inner badass. From the depths of despair, I've risen stronger and more empowered than ever before, refusing to let circumstances define my destiny. Through the trials and tribulations, I've learned valuable lessons about the importance of self-love, perseverance, and authenticity.

As I reflect on my experiences, I'm reminded of the incredible strength that resides within each of us. No matter what challenges we face, we have the power to overcome them and emerge triumphant. It's a journey of self-discovery, empowerment, and growth—a journey that requires us to dig deep into our minds, bodies, and souls to unlock our true potential.

Throughout my narrative, I've shared the raw emotions, the moments of vulnerability, and the victories that have shaped me. Each setback became a lesson, each triumph a milestone, and each step forward a testament to the resilience of the human spirit. From navigating childhood trauma to forging a path in entrepreneurship, I've learned that true empowerment comes from within—from owning our stories, embracing our vulnerabilities, and daring to be authentically ourselves.

I encourage you, dear reader, to embark on your own journey of self-discovery and personal growth. Embrace your inner badass, believe in yourself, and stay true to your authenticity. Remember that failure is not a setback but an opportunity for growth, and surround yourself with a supportive community that uplifts and empowers you.

In the end, it's not the challenges we face that define us, but how we choose to respond to them. So, as you navigate life's ups and downs, I urge you to embrace resilience, determination, and authenticity. Trust in your abilities, keep moving forward with courage and conviction, and never lose sight of the extraordinary power within you. You are capable of achieving greatness, and your journey is just beginning. Let your story be a beacon of hope and inspiration to others, showing them that no matter how dark the night may seem, there's always a glimmer of light waiting to guide them home.

Xx Nicole Curtis
Crazy Chicken Lady

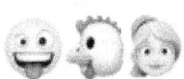

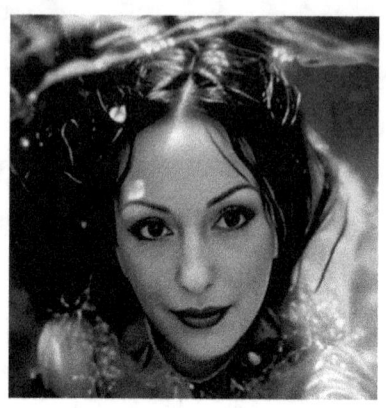

Nikki Girard

Founder and CEO of Heart Energy X Me
Quantum Resiliency Coach, Strategic Business Consulting

https://www.linkedin.com/in/nikki-girard-962601207
https://lnkd.in/ei5rMGGv
https://www.instagram.com/nikki.girard.311/
https://heartenergyxme.com/
https://www.youtube.com/@NikkiQuantum

Nikki Girard is a highly esteemed, sought after Thought Leader and Respected Authority in her field. A Quantum Resiliency Coach, and Strategic Business Consultant, making an impact & renowned for her insights, leaving clients saying, "The things Nikki knows blows my mind!" She's a Global Speaker, Amazon Bestselling - Co Author, Author of the upcoming book "High AF Advantage", & Co-Author of "Sassy Classy Badassy", sure to be on the "New York Times Bestseller List" Driven by personal experiences with traumas and adversities, Nikki's dedicated over 38 years to her passion, bridging the gap & raising the bar to achieving ultimate success in life and business. Featured publications - Pragma Journals, and Award Winning Coach - Brainz Global 500 List 2021 & Executive Contributor Brainz Magazine, along side Marisa Peer, Mel Robbins, Jim Qwik, Oprah Winfrey & more.

Nikki empowers countless individuals worldwide, with unparalleled expertise, equipping them with Quantum tools, Bending Reality, & Quantum Jumping into Limitless Possibilities.

High AF Advantage

By Nikki Girard

Your **<u>Quantum Core Blueprint</u>** to Success!!

Are you a driven individual tired of feeling stuck in your business or personal growth journey?

Want to break free from self-doubt, inconsistent results, and old patterns holding you back?

Ready to **Turbocharge** your success and embrace a life filled with positivity and purpose?

Transform your financial reality by upgrading your money codes, shattering limitations and **accessing the 95% untapped power of your brain.**

Discover how to dissolve subconscious blocks, boost productivity, and harness spiritual secrets to raise your vibration, attract abundance, creating the freedom you deserve!

Hope you like to **Rock 'n' Roll** 🎸 because in this chapter...

I'm gonna **Rock your World.**

Are you ready to unleash the fierce, unstoppable force within you and skyrocket your success?

If your answer is **"Yes"**...

Brace yourself for the game-changing...

High AF Advantage

A Strategic Insider's Guide: Unlocking Quantum Connections and Igniting your Entrepreneurial Journey through —

4 Key Pillars: *Igniting Peak Brain Performance, Flow State Sweet Spot, Cultivating Resilience and Success Mastery.*

Amplify to Multiply your Success results with more ease, expansion and inner growth…

While identifying subconscious blocks & beliefs as well as energetic blocks, unaware, holding you back from what you truly deserve in life.

Unlock your true potential by identifying hidden blocks that limit decision making.

Also discover the power of quantum jumping, to make your wildest dreams a reality!

> *"The best way to manifest something is to become a vibrational match to your own desire."* According to the *Law of Attraction teacher* — **Abraham Hicks**

The universe is your playground, and it's time to place your cosmic order for unparalleled growth, innovation, and financial freedom.

Shattering limitations and embracing limitless possibilities for a life of abundance and success.

By integrating these powerful concepts into your life, you'll become the unstoppable **"*wave*"** that defies all odds, creating a life that's as exhilarating and extraordinary as you are.

This is your moment to **Awaken the Quantum Power Ninja** *within you*, embarking on a jaw-dropping journey of self-discovery and unprecedented success.

*Transcending the illusion of the "**box**" and embracing the limitless nature of your potential, integrating…*

The **"High AF Advantage"** to create a life beyond your wildest dreams.

So buckle up and get ready for the ride of your life!!

Hello, My name is Nikki Girard,

Award Winning Coach & Entrepreneur.

Dedicated to Human Beings Wanting to Advance in Their Being, Balance & Their Ultimate Success.

Overcoming Life's Challenges We Face & Ways to Rise Above it & Grow…

For 38 plus years, My Life's Focus has been on Human Development, Consciousness, Subconscious Mind…

It's Relation to Energy

How it Works…

How it Effects Us…

And *How We Can Work with it*, towards Our Success.

Instead of Against it.

Incorporating Cutting Edge Neuroscience Advancements, Brain Neuro Plasticity, Empowerment Structuring & Resilience for Ultimate Success.

What I've learned along My Journey, through experiences, as well as 10s of thousands of hours of Researching, Training & Knowledge I've Gained…

Not Only, Unlocked the Answers…

"It Blew My Mind"

As it does with all My Clients I've worked with throughout the years.

Using Powerful Techniques, Practices and also through Empowerment Structuring, Energy Technologies, Heart Math & So Much more.

After working with people worldwide, I've created the **"High AF Advantage"** for anyone who wants to level up…

I use these *"4 pillars"* with every Client I work with, achieving Extraordinary Results.

Many coaches teach people, how to step out of their comfort zone…

I on the other hand, coach people on how to step into their comfort zone to become the best version of themselves at their highest potential for success…

Armed with…

The "High AF Advantage"

Your **Quantum Core Blueprint** *to Success!!*

* * *

Understanding the "High AF Advantage":

The *"High AF Advantage"* is a transformative concept that empowers individuals, entrepreneurs and leaders, to unlock their full potential and achieve extraordinary success.

It centers around *4 Key Pillars*: combining peak brain performance, flow state sweet spot, cultivating resilience, and success mastery.

Creating a winning formula for unparalleled growth and achievement.

At its core, the *"High AF Advantage"* focuses on optimizing mental capabilities, emotional intelligence, physical well-being and Quantum Jumping, connecting the Quantum Dots.

> *"All it takes is one moment of courage, one step forward, to change your life."* — **Mel Robbins**

The *"High AF Advantage"* optimizes personal and professional performance through energy, passion, purpose, inner drive, building resilience, lasting impact & embracing challenges.

Creating time freedom & abundance.

> *"The time is now. Stop hitting the*
> *'snooze' button on your life."* — **Mel Robbins**

Before We dig into the *4 key Pillars* of the *"High AF Advantage"*...

We will touch on a few concepts within these *4 powerful Pillars*, which incorporate additional foundational building blocks.

* * *

Building Block Fundamentals for Success:

The *"High AF Advantage"* is rooted in achieving a *"higher state of mind"* –

Fostering peak performance, flow state, resilience, and success Mastery.

This elevated mental state enables leaders to tap into their full potential, make better decisions, and navigate challenges effectively.

One essential element is understanding *"personal energy"* – recognizing the factors that boost or drain mental and physical energy.

By managing energy effectively, leaders can maintain focus, productivity, and well-being throughout their journey.

The *"High AF Advantage"* is further amplified by recognizing the *"quantum universe within"* – the vast, untapped potential that lies within each individual.

This concept encourages & *explores their inner world,* harnessing the power of thoughts, emotions, and energy to achieve extraordinary success.

While **the Law of Vibration**, **Law of Attraction**, and **Law of Manifestation** are often used interchangeably, there are subtle differences between them.

In essence,

*Key - **the Law of Vibration:***
This lays the foundation for understanding energy,

*While - **the Law of Attraction:***
It explains how this energy impacts Our experiences,

*Then - **the Law of Manifestation:***
This provides a framework for consciously harnessing these principles to create our desired reality.

*The **"quantum universe within"** is a realm of infinite possibilities, where intention and focus can shape reality.*

A key aspect of reaching this elevated mental state is **"aligning heart and brain coherence"**

When the **"heart and brain"** are in **"sync"** promoting emotional balance, mental clarity, and improved cognitive function.

This *harmony* between the **"heart and brain"** enables individuals to access their full mental and emotional resources, access to the **"Super Conscious"**

Fostering peak performance, as well as unparalleled results, faster, creating consistency & lasting impact.

The **"High AF Advantage"** synergizes energy, passion, purpose, and drive, empowering leaders to become trailblazers, achieve extraordinary success, and create exhilarating lives by embracing challenges.

The **"High AF Advantage"** embodied by *Marisa Peer, Sheryl Sandberg, and Sara Blakely.*

These women demonstrate how high aspirations and relentless drive empower women leaders to achieve extraordinary success in their fields by cultivating peak performance and resilience.

In summary, the *"High AF Advantage"* is an empowering concept that fosters peak performance and success, enabling leaders to be fueled by the cultivation of high aspirations...

Ambitious goals that push to stretch beyond their current capabilities and envision new possibilities.

* * *

1st Pillar

Igniting Peak Brain Performance

Let's take a closer look at what's happening in your brain when you are in a flow state, Igniting Peak Brain Performance and the implications.

A closer look at the brain during **Flow State** *reveals a surge in peak brain performance and productivity,* **with potential increases of up to 500%.**

This state triggers the release of performance-boosting neurochemicals like norepinephrine, dopamine, and endorphins.

Amplifying cognitive abilities and fostering compounding progress.

Just as small, consistent improvements lead to exponential growth, optimizing brain function generates momentum for extraordinary achievements.

Quantum Jumping:

This is another transformative tool that allows leaders to unleash their peak brain performance and accomplish remarkable feats.

By envisioning alternate realities where they've already achieved their aspirations, they can transcend limiting beliefs and emotional barriers.

Embracing the mindset and energy of their successful counterparts to fuel their journey towards extraordinary success.

Here are the steps for using *"Quantum Jumping"* as a guideline to achieve extraordinary results:

1. *Clarify goals:* Identify specific objectives like career milestones, personal transformation, and business growth.

2. *Visualize a successful alternate self:* Close your eyes, imagine a parallel universe where goals are achieved, and visualize this version with emotions, thoughts, and actions.

3. *Step into the role:* Mentally embody your successful self, observe their thoughts, feelings, and actions, and note insights or strategies to apply in your life.

4. *Integrate the experience:* Reflect on Quantum Jumping lessons, then identify steps to bring goals closer to reality.

5. *Embody success:* Infuse emotions and feelings as if goals are already accomplished, fostering a stronger connection with your successful alternate self.

*By incorporating **"Quantum Jumping"** leaders can tap into the full power of their minds and experience extraordinary success.*

The Energy Equation:

Energy management plays a critical role in achieving *"peak brain performance"* by *optimizing cognitive function and focus.*

It's essential to be in awareness of personal *"energy levels"* and how to maintain a balanced, sustainable *flow of energy* throughout the day.

A few key points on prioritizing activities that *boost "energy levels"* and strategies for effective energy management include:

1. *Prioritize quality sleep:* For mental clarity and overall well-being.

2. ***Practice mindfulness and stress management techniques:*** To reduce stress and improve focus.

3. ***Fuel the brain:*** With proper nutrition for sustained cognitive function.

4. ***Engaging in regular exercise:*** To enhance brain function and reduce fatigue.

5. ***Schedule breaks:*** For mental rest and rejuvenation.

By implementing targeted strategies, leaders optimize their brain performance, fueling remarkable outcomes through enhanced focus, clarity, and creativity.

Embracing the "Badass" Mindset and its connection to peak performance:

The ***"badass" mindset*** blends unwavering determination and courage, empowering women leaders to transform challenges into growth.

This mentality cultivates resilience, adaptability, and calculated risk-taking, optimizing potential and driving remarkable accomplishments.

Notable women who have embodied the ***"badass" mindset*** include:

1. ***Serena Williams:*** Unwavering determination and work ethic made her a tennis icon and advocate for gender equality and social justice.

2. ***Ruth Bader Ginsburg:*** Trailblazing late Supreme Court Justice who championed gender equality and civil rights, fueled by an unwavering commitment to justice.

3. ***Malala Yousafzai:*** Fearless and dedicated Nobel Peace Prize laureate fighting for girls' education, despite life-threatening adversity.

These women embody the *"badass" mindset*, exemplifying how determination, resilience, and commitment to excellence propel remarkable achievements and a lasting legacy.

Let's dive even deeper…

The Power of the Subconscious and Unconscious Mind:

Recent scientific studies have explored the interplay between the *"conscious"*, *"subconscious"* and *"unconscious"* mind in *shaping our thoughts, behaviors, and performance.*

Here's a closer look at these concepts and their implications for peak brain performance:

1. *The conscious mind: Encompasses present-moment awareness, including thoughts, emotions, and sensations.*

2. *The subconscious mind: Holds memories, beliefs, and habits that influence behaviors and reactions.*

3. *The unconscious mind: Consists of mental processes beyond awareness, such as autonomic functions.*

Our *subconscious* and *unconscious* minds wield significant influence over performance, shaping behaviors, decisions, and problem-solving abilities.

Deeply held beliefs, mold motivation and confidence, as the "unconscious" mind rapidly processes information, often surpassing "conscious" capabilities.

In light of these findings, several strategies leaders can employ to harness the power of their *"subconscious"* & *"unconscious"* minds:

1. *Affirmations & visualizations:* Reprogram beliefs, boost confidence, and align with goals.

2. ***Mindfulness & meditation:*** Increase awareness, uncover patterns, and improve mental clarity.

3. ***Reflection & introspection:*** Discover underlying beliefs, blocks and emotions impacting performance.

*By understanding and leveraging the power of the **"subconscious"** and **"unconscious"** minds, leaders can tap into their full potential and achieve peak brain performance.*

* * *

2nd Pillar

Mastering Flow State

*This breakdown focuses on the essential aspects of **"mastering the flow state."***

Einstein's most famous quotes about energy…

*"Energy cannot be created or destroyed,
it can only be changed from one form to another."* — **Albert Einstein**

"Everything is energy and that is all there is to it — Match the frequency of the reality you want and you can not help but get that reality. It can be no other way." — **Albert Einstein**

Mastering Flow State and the concept of ***"Become the Wave"***

"Become the Wave" promotes present-moment immersion, linking to the flow state for heightened focus, creativity, and productivity.

Energy Flows • where • Focus Goes

Leaders engrossed in tasks, access effortless concentration, navigating challenges with ease…achieving peak performance.

*"If you do what you've always done,
you'll get what you've always gotten"* — **Tony Robbins**

*"Once you have mastered time,
you will understand how true it is that most people
overestimate what they can accomplish in a year – and underestimate
what they can achieve in a decade."* — **Tony Robbins**

Adopting this mindset to enter the *"flow state"* women leaders can follow these steps:

1. *Set clear goals:* Establish well-defined objectives, provide direction and maintain motivation.

2. *Eliminate distractions:* Create an environment conducive to focus, minimizing interruptions and external stimuli.

3. *Balance skills and challenges:* Ensure tasks are aligned with your abilities, providing enough challenge to remain engaging without causing overwhelm.

4. *Cultivating mindfulness:* Practice staying present and fully engaged in the task at hand, letting go of thoughts unrelated to the activity.

When individuals "become the wave" mastering the flow state, they can tap into their full creative and problem-solving potential.

This mindset enables them to navigate challenges with greater ease, adapt to ever-changing circumstances, and achieve extraordinary success in their personal and professional lives.

Resiliency and self-mastery are also Key to overcome adversity and create a solid foundation for success mastery.

This holistic approach empowers individuals to achieve extraordinary success while maintaining their well-being and personal fulfillment.

Cultivating Resilience is the **4th Pillar,** which is discussed later in this chapter.

Let's continue...

Flow State Sweet Spot

Heart and Brain Coherence:

"Heart-brain coherence" is a state of synchronization between the heart and the brain, *where both systems work harmoniously to facilitate optimal performance.*

This coherence is essential for achieving the flow state, as it promotes mental clarity, emotional balance, and heightened intuition.

Leaders can cultivate *"Heart-brain coherence"* by incorporating strategies & techniques into their daily routines.

Embodiment is the name of the game!

Here are some approaches to foster increased coherence:

1. *Practice mindfulness meditation:* Regular meditation can enhance focus, emotional regulation, and self-awareness promoting heart-brain coherence and facilitating the flow state.

2. *Breathwork:* Deep, slow breathing exercises can synchronize heart rate variability with brainwave patterns, inducing a state of coherence and relaxation.

3. *Managing stress:* Reducing stress through exercise, hobbies, seeking support from others, helping to maintain heart-brain coherence, and preventing burnout.

4. *Positive emotion cultivation:* Cultivating positive emotions such as gratitude, love, and compassion can stimulate coherence between the heart and brain, enhancing overall well-being and performance.

5. **Work with a Coach or Mentor:** Taking you through the process step by step, with a Blueprint to Success.

"If you want to find the secrets of the universe, think in terms of energy, frequency and vibration." — **Nikola Tesla**

By prioritizing *"Heart-brain coherence"* women leaders can access the *"Flow State Sweet Spot."*

*Thus, unlocking their full potential for peak performance, creativity, resilience and **increasing productivity by up to 500%**.*

The Quantum X-Factors for Peak Performance:

Several key factors that contribute to *"peak performance"* and the *"flow state"* serve as essential components for leaders seeking extraordinary success.

Here are some *"Quantum X-Factors"* including:

1. **Clarity of purpose:** A strong sense of purpose provides direction and motivation, fueling the drive for peak performance.

2. **Laser-sharp focus:** The ability to maintain concentration and eliminate distractions is crucial for achieving the flow state.

3. **Adaptability:** Embracing change and learning from challenges promotes resilience and continuous growth.

4. **Emotional intelligence:** Self-awareness and the ability to manage emotions effectively contribute to better decision-making and leadership skills.

*By focusing on **"Quantum X-Factors"** leaders can unleash their full potential for creating a lasting impact in their respective fields.*

* * *

3rd Pillar

Cultivating Resilience

*"And the day came when the risk to
remain tight in a bud was more painful than
the risk it took to blossom."* — **Anaïs Nin**

As a resilient 17-year-old pursuing a Nursing career, I faced a life-threatening event on a stormy morning. *Struck by lightning* at the bus stop...

My arm caught fire, yet through sheer determination, I extinguished the flames and persevered.

Despite the excruciating pain, I refused to give up and completed my entire work shift at the local medical clinic.

And the running joke to this day when someone has a dead battery...

They say jokingly...I can jump it lol.

*"There is no limit to what we, as women,
can accomplish."* — **Michelle Obama**

As a Transformational resiliency coach, my stories & experience showcase human potential and inner strength.

By sharing, motivating others to overcome challenges, embracing the power within, and demonstrating that no obstacle,...

Not even a life-threatening lightning strike, can deter us from Our destined path.

*"Above all, be the heroine of your life,
not the victim."* — **Nora Ephron**

"Resilience" is essential for leaders aiming for extraordinary success.

By fostering *"resilience"* women can navigate challenges effectively and maintain their well-being.

Here are some examples of strategies for *"Cultivating Resilience"*:

1. ***Embracing challenges as opportunities for growth:*** View obstacles as opportunities, and believe in the ability to improve, grow, a chance to learn, adapt, and build resilience.

2. ***Self-Mastery:*** Prioritizing self-awareness, emotional intelligence and tapping the Super Conscious.

3. ***Work with a Mentor/Coach* or expert 1-1:** Reaching your Goals/join a course or program.

> *"We have to embrace obstacles*
> *to reach the next stage of joy."* — **Goldie Hawn**

4. ***Develop deep understanding:*** Discover personal strengths, weaknesses, values, and emotions to support resilience and self-mastery.

5. ***Engage in:*** Self-reflection, seek support and guidance, and practice mindfulness to enhance self-mastery and overall resilience.

"Cultivating Resilience" and self-mastery empower leaders to overcome challenges and build a solid foundation for success mastery.

This holistic approach fuels extraordinary success, well-being, and personal fulfillment.

Dealing with Dysregulation:

"Dysregulation" is a state of emotional, mental, or physiological imbalance caused by stress, trauma, or challenges.

This negatively impacts resilience and peak performance, reducing focus, productivity, and decision-making abilities for leaders.

To maintain resilience and high performance in the face of such challenges, leaders can employ the following strategies:

1. ***Practicing mindfulness techniques:*** *For emotional balance and mental clarity.*

2. ***Cultivate a strong support network:*** *For emotional relief and resilience.*

3. ***Prioritize self-care activities:*** *To promote well-being and counteract deregulation.*

4. ***Reframe challenges as growth opportunities:*** *To boost resilience and adaptability.*

These strategies empower women leaders to enhance resilience, manage **"*dysregulation,*"** and maintain peak performance, fueling extraordinary success amidst challenges.

Next, *"**Addressing Stored Trauma**" and its importance in building resilience.*

Addressing Stored Trauma:

"*Unresolved trauma*" from past experiences can adversely affect mental and emotional well-being, impairing resilience and peak performance.

For today's leaders, **"*addressing stored trauma*"** *is essential to overcome self-doubt, anxiety, stress & overcoming challenges.*

Several well-known women leaders have demonstrated the power of **"*addressing stored trauma*"** in pursuit of success:

- ***Maya Angelou:*** The renowned poet and author experienced childhood abuse and trauma but transformed her pain into powerful, inspiring works of literature.

- ***Elizabeth Smart:*** After enduring a traumatic kidnapping and abuse, Smart became an advocate for child safety and resilience, using her experience to empower others.

- *Arianna Huffington:* The media mogul, suffered a collapse due to exhaustion and re-evaluated her work-life balance, ultimately redefining success to include well-being and resilience.

"Addressing stored trauma" and building resilience, women leaders can:

1. *Seek professional support:* Engage in therapy or counseling to process past traumas and develop healthy coping mechanisms. Work with a Coach or Mentor, take a course or program.

2. *Practice self-compassion:* Show kindness and understanding toward Oneself, acknowledging the impact of trauma, while recognizing the resilience it took to overcome it.

3. *Share experience with others:* Connect with supportive individuals or communities to share stories, find inspiration, and foster resilience.

By confronting and "addressing stored trauma," leaders can pave the way for personal healing, enhanced resilience, and extraordinary success in their personal and professional lives.

"Maintaining a Strong Personal Foundation" *and its role in fostering resilience:*

A *"strong personal foundation"* is essential for fostering resilience, providing a solid base from which leaders can navigate challenges and pursue their high aspirations.

This encompasses self-awareness, emotional well-being, and a commitment to personal growth.

To cultivate a *robust* **"personal foundation,"** leaders can implement the following strategies:

1. **Prioritize self-care activities:** To nourish the mind, body, and spirit.

2. **Foster self-awareness:** Through journaling and self-reflection.

3. **Set boundaries:** For work-life balance and burnout prevention.

4. **Pursue continuous learning and growth:** Through workshops, reading, and mentorship.

Focusing on these strategies helps leaders develop resilience, adaptability, and peak performance.

Establishing a solid foundation for extraordinary success with lasting impact in personal and professional domains.

* * *

4th Pillar

Success Mastery

"Moving the goal post" refers to the practice of continuously setting new, ambitious goals as a means of fostering growth and success mastery.

This concept involves pushing beyond and stepping *into* one's comfort zone, *embracing challenges to unlock untapped potential.*

Success is predictable and repeatable with the **"High AF Advantage"**

> *"We will act consistently with our view of who we truly are, whether that view is accurate or not."* — **Tony Robbins**

Here are some effective steps to *"moving the goal post"* leaders can follow:

1. *Reflect on past achievements:* To identify lessons, skills, and growth areas.

2. *Set ambitious, realistic goals:* Aligned with purpose and values.

3. *Create an action plan:* With steps, resources, and strategies to overcome obstacles.

4. *Monitor progress:* Adjust as needed for continuous growth.

5. *Celebrate milestones and accomplishments:* To reinforce self-motivation.

By mastering the art of "moving the goal post," leaders can unlock their full potential and achieve extraordinary success.

This approach ensures a continual cycle of empowering growth improvement and leading to a lasting legacy of excellence.

"Women belong in all places where decisions are being made. It shouldn't be that women are the exception." — **Ruth Bader Ginsburg**

The Power of Alignment:

Women leaders attain success mastery by aligning personal and professional goals, maximizing motivation, purpose, and resilience.

This alignment optimizes resources and impact, creating synergistic outcomes that fortify resolve in the face of challenges.

Here are a few examples of successful women leaders who exemplify the *"power of alignment"* in their achievements:

1. *Marisa Peer:* Integrates her personal mission of inspiration and empowerment into professional endeavors, like her expertise in Hypnotherapy and creating her signature RTT training.

2. *Sheryl Sandberg:* Aligns professional achievements at Meta (formerly Facebook) and LeanIn.org with her personal goal of supporting women in leadership and promoting gender equality.

3. *Arianna Huffington:* Centered her professional success as a media entrepreneur, founder of Thrive Global around her personal commitment to well-being and work-life balance.

To harness *"the power of alignment"* in their own lives, women leaders can take the additional following steps:

1. *Clarify personal values and purpose:* Reflect on core values and life aspirations to identify the driving forces behind personal and professional goals.

2. *Assess current goals and priorities:* Evaluate existing objectives and commitments, ensuring they are congruent with personal values and purpose.

3. *Set aligned goals and create an action plan:* Establish new goals bridging personal and professional aspirations, and develop a *Blueprint* for achieving them.

> *"If you do what you've always done,*
> *you'll get what you've always gotten"* — **Tony Robbins**

Focusing on the *"power of alignment,"* women leaders can unleash their full potential, achieving extraordinary results while staying true to their authentic selves.

Unlocking Financial Freedom:

Financial freedom is a vital aspect of success mastery for women leaders, offering control and personal empowerment.

Achieving financial independence catalyzes growth, provides resources for personal development, and fosters opportunities for significant impact.

"Unlocking financial freedom" and leveraging it for success mastery, leaders can follow key strategies:

1. ***Enhance financial literacy:*** Understanding key concepts, and making informed decisions.

2. ***Set achievable financial goals:*** Aligned with values and success definitions.

3. ***Create a comprehensive financial plan:*** Including budgeting, saving, and investing strategies.

4. ***Diversify income streams:*** Through side business ventures, sell your digital products

5. ***Seek guidance:*** From financial professionals for strategy optimization.

6. ***Cultivate a growth mindset:*** Embracing challenges as learning opportunities on the path to financial freedom.

> *"The path to success is to take massive,*
> *determined action"* — **Tony Robbins**

By prioritizing financial freedom and adopting these strategies, leaders can unlock a world of possibilities.

Fueling success mastery and creating a lasting legacy of financial empowerment and independence.

* * *

Final Thoughts

Leveraging the "High AF Advantage"

"Embracing the High AF Lifestyle" emphasizes achieving extraordinary success while maintaining balance, well-being, and personal fulfillment.

> *"Be the change that you wish*
> *to see in the world."* — **Mahatma Gandhi**.

Gandhi's words encapsulate the essence of personal responsibility.

In a world filled with challenges, it reminds us that we have the power to initiate change by embodying the very qualities and actions we desire to witness in others.

Key aspects of the *"High AF lifestyle"* include:

1. ***Prioritizing self-care and well-being:*** Focusing on physical, mental, and emotional health to fuel personal and professional success.

2. ***Cultivating meaningful connections:*** Nurturing relationships with friends, family, and colleagues to foster support and collaboration.

3. ***Embracing lifelong learning:*** Continuously seeking new knowledge and skills to adapt to an ever-evolving world and maintain a competitive edge.

4. ***Aligning purpose and values:*** Ensuring personal and professional pursuits are congruent with core values and life aspirations.

> *"All great knowing has come from*
> *inner knowing."* — **Nassim Haramein**
> The Resonance Project • The connected universe
> • Collective Evolution

Several women leaders who exemplify the benefits of embracing the *"High AF lifestyle"*:

- ***Arianna Huffington:*** As a media mogul and wellness advocate, Huffington embodies the High AF lifestyle by emphasizing the importance of well-being, work-life balance, and personal growth.

- *Rachel Paling:* Creator of Neurolanguage & Neuroheart Education, commitment to self-improvement, aligning her work & purpose, contributing to her remarkable success and influence.

- *Sara Blakely:* The founder of Spanx, Blakely has built a thriving business while prioritizing self-care, continuous learning, and maintaining strong relationships with her team and family.

By adopting the "High AF lifestyle" leaders create a solid foundation for success mastery.

Enabling them to achieve extraordinary results while experiencing personal fulfillment and well-being.

This holistic approach ensures sustainable growth and lasting impact, empowering leaders to reach their highest aspirations.

Unlocking Limitless Potential - Leveraging the High AF Advantage:

1. *Embracing the High AF Lifestyle:* Adopt a lifestyle that emphasizes balance, well-being, meaningful connections, and lifelong learning to create a solid foundation for success mastery.

2. *Unlocking Limitless Potential:* Harness the *"High AF Advantage"* to tap into your full potential as a leader.

3. *Apply Quantum Success Principles:* Aligning personal and professional goals, fostering heart-brain coherence, and continuously refining your vision of success.

4. *Cultivate the Flow State Sweet Spot:* By managing stress, developing laser-sharp focus, and embracing adaptability. Perspective is Adaptive.

5. *Focus on self-mastery and resilience:* By engaging in self-reflection, seeking support, and fostering a growth mindset.

"You are the universe looking back at itself and learning about itself." — **Nassim Haramein**

Unlock your limitless potential with the *"High AF Advantage"*

Embracing transformative strategies to achieve extraordinary success, inspire others, and pave the way for a world of empowered leaders.

Take action today…

Invest in you and your future…

Be on the cutting edge of Business & Personnel Development…

Quantify your Success…

Shatter Limitations…

Witness the life-changing power of manifestation, as you…

Connect the Quantum Dots *with…*

The *"High AF Advantage"*

Rock & Roll 🎸 *your way to the top!*

* * *

Again,

I'm *Nikki Girard,*

Transformational Quantum Resiliency Coach & Strategic Business Consultant

I've already done the heavy lifting, so you don't have to…

Let's do this together…

Fast-track your Success…

I've got your back…

So Let's Goooo!!

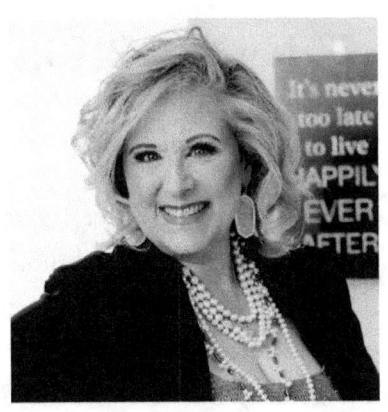

Renee Ozier

Founder of The Next Step- with Neuro-Coach/
Consultant Renee Ozier

https://www.linkedin.com/in/renee-o-43535ba5/
https://tinyurl.com/reneeozierfacebook
https://tinyurl.com/reneeozierinstagram
https://www.thenextstepcoach.com

Renee Ozier is a lifelong educator, former school principal, trainer, neuro-coach, speaker, writer, and retreat leader! She combines GRIT with GROWTH opportunities, and GOD to facilitate lasting transformations for women in their 2nd half of life- to make it their BEST HALF OF LIFE! Today, Renee is a full-time neuro-coach... coaching women who are experiencing significant life transitions that produce uncertainty, upheaval, fear, or scarcity. Her clients come away with skills to successfully rewire their brains, mend broken beliefs, transform their results, change their limiting mindsets, and prepare them for greater success and joy! Renee helps women reframe, refocus, re-purpose, and renew their God-given talents, abilities, and genius to help them create their NEXT STEP in life! Renee is most proud and blessed to hold the title of "Mom" to her 6 children and "Nana" to her 7 grandchildren who are the "loves of her life!"

Girls with GRITS!

By Renee Ozier

Growing up in the Southwest, grits were a staple food at any good Southern table, especially for breakfast and brunch! Grits are ground hominy, made delicious and creamy with the addition of water or milk and loads of butter and even cheese! Every good southern mamma serves grits with most meals...and it was a necessity in my house growing up with my father, who insisted grits were part of the daily menu!

However, at first glance, the word GRITS can represent *Girls Rock in Texas with Sass and Sparkle!* And while that is most definitely true in my experience- GRITS stands for so much more than a "regional nod" to the southern cuisine or the spunky, sparkling, unabashedly fun and proud gals of our Southwestern bluebonnet laden Lone Star State! True, Texans sometimes have the reputation of being "larger than life," which translates to "Sassy, Classy, and Badassy!" "Don't Mess with Texas"- or better yet- "Don't Mess with Texas Gals"- another clichéd statement about the strong, proud, sassy, classy, and badassy ladies inhabiting this great state! Yes, Texans may brag about their state and their people- but in my experience, it's the WOMEN of this state that genuinely exemplify the sassiness that goes along with our true Texas GRITS!

Well, already I have a confession...I'm not a native Texan! I was born in Anchorage, Alaska, in 25 BELOW 0 weather! I love the cold and snow, and Lord only knows how I put up with the sizzling, hot, sticky summers of 110 degrees each year! But Texas is where I have made my home for the last four decades and where I raised my six children- and I am sure that I can now say with certainty that I am a true Texas Girl with Texas-sized GRITS!

But as I stated in the beginning, GRITS means so much more to me than just a descriptive acronym for the "sassy, classy, and badassy" girls of Texas!

GRITS, at its finest and best, represents five key qualities of ladies that reside anywhere in the country or, in fact, the world at large! True GRITS can be found in all four corners of the globe and can be inherited as qualities simply passed down from generation to generation. As well, or more importantly, GRITS can be "caught and taught!"

Girls with GRITS carry GRACE, RESILIENCE, INTEGRITY, TENACITY, and SASS or SPARKLE in their very souls! These qualities can appear at a very young age or be acquired throughout a lifetime of experiences, journeys, and lessons learned. Most often, these four qualities show themselves in those women who have experienced a well-lived life filled with determination and the backbone needed to withstand and survive the strong winds of an adventurous and sometimes treacherous journey through life!

To illustrate the principles of GRITS, I would like to share with you, my reader, part of my own story of broken to blessed, victim to victor, and survivor to thriver. However, initially, it bears mentioning the stories of two other women in my life who showed me what true GRITS looked like and who fully embodied the qualities of being "sassy, classy, and badassy!"

Lorraine Marie Wiliams, my mother, God rest her soul, was a true sassy, classy, and badassy woman with an extra helping of Texas GRITS! The story of my mother, a girl who happened to have landed in Texas, began in Tulsa, Oklahoma, where she lived out the first part of her life. She made it through Catholic girls' school and most of college but had to leave in her senior year and forgo the ability to graduate to move back home to take care of her mother, who had some severe health issues. She could never complete her degree and went to work soon after to help support the family! My mother was a uniquely classy woman who never showed herself without being dressed to the nines. She preferred lasting quality to trendy fashion and was never seen as anything but a true lady! In her earlier years, she had aspirations of becoming either a religious sister in a convent or an actress on stage and screen! However, those two pathways never materialized for her, and she chose the life of "wife and mother" to fulfill her most pressing dream of having a child and becoming a mother! Sadly, like many women today, she found herself not in the marriage that she had hoped for but rather in a difficult marriage with a very controlling spouse, my father, who was emotionally traumatized from his past and who could not show up for her in an emotional capacity. My father was a good man, to be sure- but he was impossible to relate to, to converse with, or to dream with. He was a retired Colonel in the Air Force, and it was his way or the highway! She could never be herself, and her inner light struggled to shine! Yet, she never lost faith in her God or her strength of character. She began several businesses, worked as an entrepreneur for a bit, worked with my father in his real estate business, and managed to hold firm to her highest and most loved role of all that of mother and "nana!" Although she survived a home life of perpetual fighting, emotional discord, and dryness in her marriage, she never gave up and never lost hope that her life would have meaning. She focused all her strength and energy on me and only dreamed of passing along her spirit and faith to me, her only child and the daughter she had prayed for! This was not the healthiest of situations for her or for me, as there was tremendous pressure to be the sole focus of her life's energy. Yet, she was a fortress of strength- even during the most challenging times in her marriage and in our home life, where nothing existed but sadness, disillusionment, and trauma. The marriage had been the wrong match from the beginning, but she held to her convictions of raising a child in a home that was not broken by divorce...Was this the best answer?

In my eyes, it was not- but my mother was tenacious in her beliefs, and no one could sway her otherwise!

If I heard it once, I heard it a thousand times... She would say to me... "It's a poor ball that can't bounce twice!" This is where my GRITS originally started- with the "poor ball" analogy! I was allowed to get down, but I learned the value of not STAYING down for long!

My mother, Lorraine, was the classiest, best dressed, toughest, and most resilient lady of grace and tenacity that anyone had ever known! She carried herself with such a demeanor of elegance at all times- even in the last years of her life, stricken with cancer. She died early on in my married life- however, she at least had several years with most of my six young children to bond with them, love them with a crazy passionate love, and nurture them in the same way that she nurtured me. She passed along to them through her example of GRITS- her sense of grace, resilience, integrity, tenacity, and sass and sparkle! All six of my children possess the key qualities of GRITS- simply because they saw it modeled for them at a very early age- as did I!

From her, I refined my sense of passion and purpose and drew such wisdom and acceptance to journey onward in my life!

My mother taught me several valuable lessons about Girls with GRITS- not through her words - but through her way of living and being, which showed me that GRITS meant more than Girls Rock in Texas Sassy and Sparkling... GRITS truly embodied these five words- GRACE, RESILIENCE, INTEGRITY, TENACITY, and SASS!

Aside from my mother, one other person in my life taught me about GRITS and grace! Dawn was my theater professor at Northwestern, where I was a newly married undergrad. She first became my mentor there and soon became one of my closest friends in life! She was a true Texas girl at heart with a soul filled with GRITS! She was just one of those friends- the kind you find but once in a lifetime...but God, she had GRITS oozing from her pores, infusing all she did, all she said, all she wore, and all she stood for! She found fun in any situation- laughing out loud, wearing her big jewelry, her cowboy boots, and her huge, sassy smile! She loved life and her family and friends more passionately and more completely than anyone I have ever known! She too, struggled with her home life in so many ways- especially in her marriage! She lived a full life, but her life was filled with so many emotional twists and turns, like so many of us experience. Dawn did struggle in her life, like so many of us do, with finances, relationships, self-esteem, etc... But because of her own mother, who was a "Texas gal" herself and endowed with a lively sense of GRITS- Dawn was able to tap into that strength and develop the traits necessary to withstand and overcome the traumas and the setbacks that she herself experienced! But she loved her family, her amazing son, her only brother, her nieces and nephews, and the memory of her beautiful sister and mother who had both gone to be with Jesus years before. Like my mother, Dawn threw herself wholeheartedly into her profession as an acting coach and tenured professor at Northwestern, but especially into her role as mother to a precious young son- the light and the love of her life! I never saw her death coming- as I was with her only a few short weeks before she suddenly passed away from cancer- a disease that none of us knew she had and one she fought back valiantly until the end! I was able to record a message for her on my phone, and her sweet son was able to play that message out loud for her as she lay dying. I was unable to be present at her side, as my son was getting married in Colorado that same weekend. However, I will always cherish the last weekend we spent together at her home- reminiscing and laughing until our sides hurt! She tried to give me so many of her belongings to take home with me- and I kept turning her down, saying that I could get them the next time we visited together. Somehow, she must have known this would be our last time together...The day she took me to the train station to head back to Chicago to be with one of my sons, she hugged me tighter than ever before, and as the train pulled away- I caught a glimpse of her running alongside it- screaming, "I love you honey" at the top her lungs...It would be the last image I had of her. Thank God I had that time with her that weekend...to drink in her love and her passion for life!

Like my mother, Dawn always showed up dressed to impress, of course- but more than that, she showed up ready to embrace those she valued and loved. They both had a unique way of making you feel as if you were the only person on the planet! They would have walked through fire to defend their beliefs and to defend those they loved! They both had more GRITS and gumption than any movie heroine I have ever watched! From gun-toting gals to determined businesswomen, my mother, Lorraine, and my dear friend Dawn put Annie Oakly, Thelma and Louise, Norma Rae, Erin Brockovich, Dolly Parton, Carrie Bradshaw and girls from Sex and the City, Sally Field, and Charlie's Angels to shame!

What two incredible role models I had in my earlier years to watch, emulate, and live up to! Little did I know that these two Girls with GRITS- would fortify me to withstand and emerge from one of the darkest and most devastating times in my life.

In my late 30's, I suddenly found myself alone. My father had died of heart failure in the year 2000, my husband of almost 20 years had decided to leave our marriage the day after my father's death, and my mother received a devastating diagnosis of pancreatic cancer shortly thereafter! She lived only a short nine months after her diagnosis! I had six children (ranging in ages from 2 to 12, the last two being identical twin boys) to raise, and I had no income because I had been a homeschooling stay-at-home mother for the last two decades of my life. I dealt with bankruptcy following divorce, impending foreclosure, and the start of a new career all at the same time. I had to turn to a career that would mesh with my children's school schedules- now that they had to re-enter traditional schooling- since I was no longer able to homeschool them because I had to work and make an income in order for all of us to survive!

Because of my own troubled childhood trauma of growing up with an emotionally difficult father and a home that was chronically filled with fighting, tension, and discord… I had always been a sickly young adult and child- dealing with IBS and colitis, migraines, and an anxiety disorder. I had learned how to somewhat navigate life and survive with these chronic conditions, but now had to do so with no backup parent, spouse, or family member to help when the going got tough! I was an only child, and both of my parents had recently died; I had very little family that I could turn to, so I turned to God! My love of my faith had always been strong, and Jesus and I always had a relationship. But now, it had to be different and more intensely intimate! Through prayer and petition, God helped me get through each day- sometimes just one moment at a time. He helped me raise my children, trust Him, and take those next right steps in life that he was laying before me! It is true… Like the song says, "God DOES bless the broken road" before us if we turn to Him, listen, obey, and act! He strengthened me through those life challenges that I have only glossed over here for the sake of brevity. If I wasn't a girl with GRITS beforehand- I certainly had become one now!

I did survive and ultimately found a way to thrive!

I continued to teach and found time to obtain my master's degree in educational administration. I went on to lead several schools as the school principal and campus leader. Although I continued to struggle in relationships with abusive men over the years- I ultimately worked through my fears and my lack of self-worth following the traumatic divorce that I had endured. It took many years, but the journey to discover my worth and my purpose was ultimately very worth the effort and time! I now have been privileged to retire from education and begin work as a transformational neuro-coach, coaching women in their second half of life as they struggle to navigate their way through life changes, divorces, death of loved ones, moves, career upheavals, financial loss and so much more! My Next Step, neuro-coaching/consulting/speaking/retreat business, continues to grow and flourish because I took the time to conquer my fears, change my brain and my thoughts, erase limiting beliefs that kept me stuck in a negative self-image and created new neural pathways that paved the way for me to experience success and growth like never before! I married a kind and caring man- who allowed me the time and space to grow through all of these stages, and I now have a thriving business and I feel like I have finally arrived in the land of my true purpose! Yet, without acquiring the tenets of true GRITS, I would not have ventured to change my life and grow in ways that would one day set me up to step into my true purpose and calling. I relied on the GRACE I needed to carry on in times of stress and distress, the RESILIENCE of that ball that HAD to bounce twice in life and keep on bouncing for the sake of my children, the INTEGRITY that I had to show during the hardest and darkest days as I struggled as a single mother and which was gifted to me through my strong faith in God and the strong role models I had, the TENACITY to carry on in the face of setbacks so that I could eventually set my life up for a comeback and for transformational success and finally, the SASS and SPARKLE that lived within my soul and drove me to be sassy yet classy throughout my ordeals!

That is just an important point...although I have illustrated several examples of GRITS coming from watching and learning from other Girls with GRITS...GRITS does not have to be a "generational" gift coming from a role model and mentor! GRITS are available to us ALL! GRITS can as easily be formed and nurtured through the adoption of a set of life traits and characteristics that can be cultivated, studied, and developed through diligence, determination, and desire!

So how can YOU benefit from the stories I have told, the ladies I have brought to life for you, and the lessons I have learned along the way? How can you, too, refine and sharpen these characteristics that define GRITS and become an unstoppable Girl with GRITS??

I want to remind you what virtues the word GRITS represents and then offer you four key takeaways about how to recognize and refine your own sense of GRITS!!

G=Grace R=Resilience I=Integrity T=Tenacity S= Sass and Sparkle

G=Grace. Girls with GRITS exhibit grace and class in all situations. Revenge and getting even have no place in the Girl with GRITS. Forgiveness, a sense of calm confidence, and elegance travel with her and are some of the key traits of a Girl with GRITS!

R=Resilience. Girls with GRITS don't stay down for long! They may get the wind knocked out of them- but they breathe, recover, and get back up to face the next hurdle with determination and a fierce inner drive!

I=Integrity. Girls with GRITS do the right thing because it is the right thing to do! They do what is moral and just- even when no one is looking. They have to live with themselves, and they possess a king-sized conscience that dictates their actions and integrity toward others. They may not always be treated fairly or with respect...but they certainly do not do the same in return. As Mother Teresa always said... "People will be unkind- but be kind anyway. In the end, it is not between you and them- it is between you and God!"

T=Tenacity. Girls with GRITS are like bulldogs with a bone...They are as ferocious as a lioness protecting her cubs, and nothing stops them for long! They may get lost, stumble, and even fall occasionally- but their tenacity and willfulness always lift them back into a standing position- ready to go for round two! Rocky Balboa has nothing on Girls with GRITS!

S= Sass and Sparkle. Girls with GRITS develop an inner "sass" that allows no one to put them in a corner for long or under a doormat to be walked on and abused! Girls with GRITS may struggle with hard times, bad relationships, doubts, and fears- but their small inner voice always shows up eventually, reminding them that they are "badass, sassy, sparkling" women who deserve to be loved, valued, and respected!

HOW CAN YOU, TOO, BE A GIRL WITH GRITS?

1. _Girls with GRITS possess that Texas-sized sense of purpose and absolute unwillingness to bend in their determination, which is one reason they will only become stronger in the wake of adversity or challenge._ As evidenced in the stories of Dawn, my mother, and myself- Girls with GRITS are able to forge ahead in the wake of the dissolution of life as they know it… They are able to stay focused on their end goal by being vigilant and unwilling to break in the face of a setback! This is a CHOICE you can make…no matter the circumstance! You will simply "DIA"…DECIDE IN ADVANCE…DO IT ANYWAY…. And DECIDE- INITIATE- and ACT!!! However you break this down and define it- DIA allows you to make a plan, work that plan, and complete that plan! This can be done with a coach, an accountability partner, a group, or a support network. DIA is a staunch adherence to your planned agenda each day, repetition, practice, and strict adherence to weeding through any negative input in your thinking and thought patterns. It is being willing to work with a coach, mentor, partner, etc….. to rewire and refocus your thought patterns towards overcoming broken beliefs and ultimately towards BEING that healthy and capable woman who is capable of achieving unlimited success in her life!

2. _Girls with GRITS will lick their wounds and maybe spend a day or two giving in to the pity party they are throwing_

themselves...but watch out on day three! I know that there were tremendous setbacks in the lives of both women I spoke about and for myself. I can tell you that I suffered from intense moments of despair in those darker days following the loss of my parents and the loss of my marriage- but I felt I had no choice but to get back up on that proverbial horse and continue to gallop ahead with my children watching me and watching how I handled the challenges that presented themselves! How do Girls with GRITS get back up? As Nike says... "They just DO IT!" Again, it is a choice to stay down, to wallow, to ignore tasks at hand. As hard and harsh as it seems- just taking one step at a time and one moment at a time moves that needle and puts you back in the game! How do you eat an elephant? One bite at a time...Consistently and continuously!

3. *Girls with GRITS will not stand for their spirits to be caged for long... They will not allow their diamonds- their sparkling gems of wisdom and genius- to go unpolished!* For Girls with GRITS, it is more about "being" than doing... They will focus on their spirit, their faith, and their beliefs...and they will not stand for anyone to "cage" and hinder their areas of genius and wisdom! They will not only *do* what is needed to move that needle, but they will *become* the best version of themselves- they will uncover their diamonds underneath, in the recesses of their being, that will allow them to sparkle and shine in their life! They will uncover their resolve, their determination, their hopes for the future, their dreams, and their goals. Girls with GRITS will focus on the large window in front of their faces and refuse to continue looking back in the rearview mirror! The front window is large, and the rearview mirror is small in comparison for a reason! We are meant to look ahead, to see what's coming up, to have a broad vision for our future...We

are not meant to keep straining our necks to look behind us and try and make out the images in that tiny, small rearview mirror- the images that we have chosen to leave behind!

4. *Girls with GRITS know the sense of obligation they feel to themselves and their tribe- a sense that runs deeper than their Texas-sized sense of pride - it's the call of PURPOSE!*

Yes ma'am… My tribe was my six children- and the sense of obligation I felt to them was indescribable! I was not going down without a fight! I vowed to somehow continue to draw upon that sense of GRITS that I had witnessed early on in my life from my mother and from my amazing friend, Dawn! They both showed me how to carry on through life's trials while avidly pursuing their individual purposes. I, too, had heard the call of PURPOSE, and I needed to answer that call! Yes- I was that ball that continued to bounce- over and over again through divorce, deaths, illnesses, bankruptcy, loss of financial stability, low income, and continual moves with my children. I never had enough money at the time to afford a downpayment in order to purchase a home- so we rented all those years and moved over and over again when rents were raised and finances could not support the increase! However, teaching and education were the right fit for me at the time because my work schedule could mesh with my children's school schedules, and I was not forced to leave them unattended for long periods of time!

Over the years, as my children all grew up and fled the nest to make their own way in life, I closed a chapter in education and worked on my new purpose - to become a neuro-coach,   coaching women along their journeys who are experiencing much of what I had already lived through and overcame! I have been a coach and speaker and am now working on building life-changing retreats for women and becoming a published author!

Yet none of what I have survived would have become a story of thriving had it not been for the Girl with GRITS that I became early in life! For that, I owe my success and my future to Jesus, my confidant, and my most encouraging supporter! He was my co-parent and co-pilot as I raised my children as a single mother with little extended family nearby. As well the lessons I learned from my mother and from Dawn taught me the value of always being a Girl with GRITS- being a girl exuding GRACE and class through any circumstances, being RESILIENT and sassy enough to continue to get back up no matter what life hands you, showing INTEGRITY in all situations and acting from a place of virtue, being overwhelmingly TENACIOUS and never giving up, and finally showing SASS and SPARKLE through it all, being proud of being your authentic self, knowing your own worth, and exuding sassiness yet classiness! A sassy and sparkling woman never gives in to overwhelming challenges and difficulties…She recognizes her broken beliefs, rides out her challenges, learns from her mistakes, conquers her fears, and moves that needle! She shows what being totally "badassy" is all about!

You can never count Girls with GRITS out! They really are the balls that DO BOUNCE TWICE!

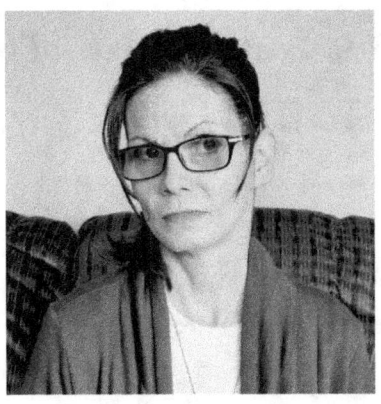

Robin Lashinski

Writer

https://www.facebook.com/Robinklammmer
https://www.instagram.com/robinklammer
https://robinklammer.medium.com/

Robin Klammer, in a nutshell; A forlorn mid-life writer gal, born and raised in Alberta, who is writing a brand new chapter in her story. She loves music such as the Blues, Bluegrass, Spanish, Arabic, Classical and more. Robin feels most at home with nature, animals and great friends. Writing is her soul's way of offering a smile or hope to people when they need it most, along with humour, however macabre it may be. Robin Klammer is found lurking on Facebook as @Robin Klammer. She has also been included in many anthologies such as Social Justice Inks. Words To Light Your Way Home is her own collection of poetry and prose, written in a raw, relatable way of how depression impacts your life, your friends and family. Robin offers up a dollop of humour and hope in her writing on Medium. You can find her as medium.com/@robinklammer

I Once Was Lost, But Now I'm Found: All I Had To Do Was Look in a Mirror.

By Robin Lashinski

I looked in the mirror and I didn't recognize myself. Where did that spunky gal go? She was long gone, or perhaps some remnants were lying dormant. I was desperate to find one burning ember from my former self. However dim it was if indeed it was still flickering, there was hope and I clung to it with a vice-like grip.

Imagine my indignation at where I was in my life. A life based on lies, lies, and more lies. Lies concocted not because I wanted to go along with them, but ones I went along with after much browbeating and coercion. Lies that if found out could have far-reaching consequences.

I felt as though I was living in a house of cards that might collapse at any moment. The stress of it all was more than I could bear. All because HE wanted to save money.

Granted, he was good at saving money, but at whose expense? The effects it was having on me were surely taking its toll, but any time I wanted to make things right, I was told I was paranoid.

"Just take it easy!" HE said. Sure, no biggie! I don't mind living with a nervous system that has been hijacked since forever.

A long tale of unfortunate events if ever there was one. If you're familiar with Seinfeld, then you might say I was all the characters combined. However, I related to George Costanza the most; though Kramer and Seinfeld were equally close second. I must say; I definitely take after Elaine in the love department or lack thereof.

Back to reality…

I was the one who swore she would never tolerate a man treating her as an afterthought or a nuisance rather than an equal partner who was loved and accepted as she was.

Who the hell was I anyway? I didn't know anymore. The person I was before I became involved with my ex of 25 years had essentially died, or at the very least, was on life support.

Speaking of which, all I could think of was death.

How would I do it?

What was the best way to die without it looking like I had committed the mortal sin of murder? It would be my own murder, though. No one else's. Just li'l ol' me. I had sunk so low I no longer felt human. Sure, I looked human, but I was simply an empty vessel with little to offer my family. My cup was empty, and I was in the Sahara Desert of relationships. I had nothing left to give, and my soul was barren.

So consumed with death was I, that I had since neglected any semblance of any true self-care. Why bother? I hated what I had become. I didn't see the point of my life anymore, aside from the obligatory showers and other absolute basics which were a feeble attempt, at best, to feel semi-normal. I felt anything but human, though. It took a Herculean effort to do the most basic things back in those days.

I researched ways to do the deed, but I wanted a guarantee that it would work. If I ended up a vegetable, then I'd be an even bigger burden on my family than I already was. And believe me, it was implied on a regular basis that I was indeed a burden.

Don't you feel all warm and fuzzy right now? I'm just about to break into my own rendition of kumbaya.

So, how would I escape from the despair and rage that I was imprisoned in? Could I actually do it? I wasn't sure. I had written my goodbye letters, asking my family not to hate me and that I was sorry. I just couldn't live like this anymore.

I certainly wouldn't be the first in my family to make this dramatic exit from life. A great-grandfather and an uncle had both made this tragic decision when the pain became too great for them; not to mention other family members who also faced suicidal ideation at times when faced with crippling depression.

I often imagined I was cursed by family ghosts. One of them is my grandmother from my mother's side of the family. My youngest uncle was also plagued by depression. There was so much heartache and dysfunction in my family.

That being said, if I accepted this fate in life, then was I destined for misery in perpetuity? That meant I had no choices in my life, no choice in my destiny. What kind of life was that? I had encased myself in a victimhood mentality for as long as I could remember; I hated the sound of my "woe be me" swan song. Something had to give.

How would my youngest child react to his mother being gone? As children are wont to do, they believe they are the cause of anything bad that happens. "If only I'd been a better kid, then mom (or whomever) wouldn't have done such and such, and so it goes. Sending a ripple effect down the line that we can never anticipate. I think my youngest son was the only reason I hung on for so long, but that didn't stop me from thinking about death constantly.

No matter how much I kept thinking of how to do the deed, I just couldn't go through with it. After all, wouldn't I be the biggest hypocrite ever if I did the deed? After waxing poetic in a book about not giving up no matter what. No matter how bad things were. I needed to take my own advice to heart.

While I didn't know exactly what my purpose in life was, I knew it involved writing and lifting people up in their worst moments. Who was I to turn my back on that? Or my kids? My mom and many others whom I had cut out of my life?

I knew all too well that life throws the ultimate curveballs at you when you least expect it.

A dear friend of mine was dealing with two kinds of cancer, and I was living over 3,000 kilometers away. It broke my heart that he was going through cancer treatment alone and dealing with very stressful life events on top of the cancer because, hey, why not, right?

A grim thought occurred to me. What if I had cancer? Would I be seen as even more of a burden? Would I still have to deal with the regular house chores while going through treatment? I mean, it's no big deal, right? Don't be such a wuss!

Did I really want to live the remainder of my life in this misery? If not, what was I going to do about it? I didn't know yet... but something had to give.

In January of 2022, we escaped from our teeny, tiny northern Ontario town of Manitouwadge and flew to Turkiye, formerly known as Turkey. Because hey, what else do you do when your relationship has imploded? You flee the country!

However, I had not anticipated the barrage of emotions I would encounter upon arrival. The vast differences of the culture and the language barrier sent me running for the hills.

Don't get me wrong though, as much as I was adrift in my own sorry-ass life, I soon embraced the country, at least in the part I lived in, and its quirks. I hope to return there in the future but on my own terms.

As much as I loved the Mediterranean Sea, I had an unhealthy obsession with the ocean. It was a mere few blocks away from the complex in Kestel, Alanya, where we lived. I would often imagine walking into the ocean fully clothed and letting the current take me away.

Or perhaps I'd find a cliff to launch myself off into the sea. Who knew where I might wash up? But again, I'd think of my son.

Thoughts of death would often plague me from morning til night.

Anyway, back to planning my demise.

I have a congenital condition called hypothyroidism, which wreaks havoc on your body if you don't adhere to the right dose of daily medication. I thought I would save whatever medication I could, take them all at once, and cause myself a heart attack, but I didn't know how much, so cue the scratch on those good old nostalgic records. Remember those?!

Another alternative was the anti-depressants I had. Perhaps, they would be a good second choice, but again, no guarantees. I had no clue what the side effects would be if I survived.

I had only one mission: To get through whatever days I had left until such time I could carry out my plan.

I often wonder how many people understand just how complex depression is. If I may add this little tidbit? Depression is a whole-body experience. It's not just in your head. I'll tell you that much right now. It's a whole-body thing, for lack of a better word.

And by the way? If you have moderate to severe depression? The worst antidote ever is apathy and/or toxic positivity.

If you or a loved one has never experienced moderate to severe depression, then thank your lucky stars! Because frankly, I wouldn't wish it on my worst enemy. Really and truly.

To have a partner who was completely unaware of the consequences of how he treated you, or simply didn't care?

To be constantly gaslit, undermined, dismissed, and ridiculed to the point you would rather be dead?

When your partner tells your child not to listen to his own mother? What kind of toll do you think that takes upon you?

When your child defers to their dad all the time because he's been heavily influenced by his father?

It seems I had no hand in raising my son who was fast approaching adolescence. What kind of man would he become? That's what scared me the most, and it still does. Toxic masculinity ran rampant in our household. No mistake about it. I hoped and prayed my son wouldn't adopt this line of thinking, but at the time, it seemed he only needed me when he wanted food or something along those lines.

The baby I nursed far longer than I ever anticipated was becoming like his dad in no uncertain terms. How did this happen?

I was beginning to look at my son and his dad as a tag team of bullies who conspired against me. When in the midst of a Dark Night of the Soul, your perspective may be way off, or it you might be seeing things exactly as they are, and as hard as you might try to reconcile this dreary reality, you'd be hard pressed to make much sense of this life you're entrenched in. All you can think of is the sweet relief you'd have if you made your premature exit. But then guilt would wash over me at the thought of leaving my son behind.

I was in quite the pickle. I didn't know how to live, or how to die. All I wanted was for the mental/emotional pain to stop.

It was apparent that any thoughts or feelings of mine were considered… an irritant, at best.

God forbid, I might be a wet blanket upon his delusional way of life. After all, I should never veer away from fluffy bunnies and/or unicorns flying out of my arse!

Bitter much? Why no, no, I'm not! LOL. The biggest lie of the century.

Anyway…

Was there any purpose to my life other than servitude? To cook, clean, and be a servant?

Before I happened upon Dr Ramani's YouTube channel, I thought there was something fundamentally flawed about me. After all, that's all I ever heard. I could never compare to his mother or sisters or other women in that culture.

I didn't do this enough, or I wasn't selfless enough. I didn't give enough, etc.

Please hear me when I tell you this.

If you have to change yourself to be with someone else, then you're with the wrong person. Full stop.

Everything was always my fault. There was no accountability on his part. EVER. I wonder

if he ever had any clue how much he hurt me. Did he care? My guess? Probably not.

My partner and I were from very different cultures. He was from the Middle East, and I am from Canada… eh?! Suffice it to say, we had had a very different mindset as to relationships and raising children. While we had a similar outcome in mind, we had very different methods of the actual discipline of how children should be raised. This was a constant bone of contention.

Since I was essentially raised in foster care off and on since infancy (by the way, not my choice, as if it ever was), HE considered me a barbarian or heathen of sorts.

Yeah, foster care with strangers beats familiarity any day of the week!

Especially, when it happens on a semi-regular basis, as in every couple of years.

I loved being away from my family. Mainly my mom. Sure, I loved to be isolated, insulted, bullied, and so on in the foster/group homes I lived in during my youth.

I was accused of having no family values, while he gave himself a big pat on the back for his family values.

Sure… why not! I always love a good laugh! You remember this is me, right? The one who is always watching and listening to the conflicting words vs actions. I absorbed the utter hypocrisy I witnessed on a daily basis.

Anyway…

So yes, I have issues. Surprise, surprise! And guess what? I brought a whole shitload with me into our relationship. Last time I checked, there weren't too many people without a few issues in their life.

Granted, some are far less harrowing than others, but we all have emotional baggage whether we admit it to ourselves or not.

Oh, and throw in the merciless bullying at school with very few teachers who don't care enough to intervene, or ask how you're really doing.

Truth be told; I never felt like I belonged anywhere. Family was a giant cluster f#ck in my neck of the woods, Alberta that is.

And here I was trying to make things in my family work, whatever the hell that meant. All the while facing the same issues I did in childhood with my partner. Was I missing something crucial?

Oh right, maybe going back in time and never meeting him in the first place. Although, that would mean my children wouldn't exist… Shit!

Ok, never mind. This is all rhetorical, since there are no time machines that I'm aware of.

After you have the same argument with your partner over the course of several years, and nothing changes or is resolved? This might mean you're simply with the wrong person.

Or if they're telling you all the things that are wrong with you, yet refuse to hear what you might like for them to change, or fly into a rage? This is indicative of your future together years down the road.

Are you prepared to be very unhappy for the rest of your life, or at the very least, for several more years?

Ask yourself this question: Do you feel relieved when they're not in your presence?

Be as honest as you can with yourself. After all, it's your life we're talking about here. Are there children involved?

Do you want them to grow up thinking, "This is what love looks like?"

To say I'm analytical to a fault would be like saying, "The sky is blue today."

Yup, no shit Sherlock!

How can you possibly make things work when you have very little to no say in your own life?

We lived in relative isolation for most of our relationship, and when our kids started school, especially our daughter, our conflicts became much more intense.

My autonomy and/or any semblance of authenticity was stripped from me. Not all at once, mind you, it happened so gradually that I couldn't quite put my finger on it. I just knew something was very wrong.

I tried in vain to make things work until I finally gave up.

A life in perpetual isolation where my thoughts and feelings were dismissed and ridiculed unless they were in line with what HE wanted. Go along to get along. Guess what? It doesn't work, not even remotely.

I tried in vain to appease him, but to no avail.

I was usually made the villain and/or scapegoat since I had no clue of how families worked.

While I may have had trust issues in regards to people from growing up in care, I craved a sense of connection. I wanted to belong somewhere. Anywhere.

While I was in Alanya, I craved a connection with people I met, especially, the social group on Facebook which gathered twice a week in Alanya. I realized how much I missed being around people from all walks of life   . Man or woman, it didn't matter.

Well, not to me. My ex, however, didn't want me hanging out with them because they weren't good people. And how would he know this exactly? It's not like he ever spent any time with them. But when he wanted answers to questions about life in Alanya, he had no scruples about asking these very same people. His utter hypocrisy never ceased to amaze me.

Please hear me out on this one message, if you hear nothing else.

If you have to change yourself to be with someone? It's NOT worth it. Believe me when I say, you're in for a lifetime of misery. I learned the hard way, so please save yourself and your children the time, heartache, and grief.

You don't know what you don't know until you know. Then you'll wonder how you didn't see the signs. They're not always obvious, that's for sure.

How did I get here, anyway? Why did I give up my autonomy? Why was I so desperate to cling to a charade of a family in which I had absolutely no say?

My goals of writing were considered a silly hobby at best. I wasn't being realistic. It was simply a waste of time and effort. Plus, if I wasn't making any money, then I was wasting everyone's time. He always wanted me to know my worth to him. A big fat zero, in no uncertain terms.

He would always deny his mistreatment of me, which led me to doubt my sanity even more.

When you crush someone's spirit on a daily basis, what do you think will happen? When you control every aspect of your partner and child's life? Eventually, there's going to be some kickback… or in my case? A shit ton.

I'd had enough of this BS! I had nothing left to lose, so I went from a meek angry mouse to a raging bitch. No bars held. This was in the last several months we were together.

I started calling him out on his ideologies, and doing little experiments to test my theories from Dr. Ramani's channel, and was surprised and disgusted when he reacted in the way the doctor predicted.

I decided to ramp it up a few notches, just to see what would happen. There was no domestic violence unless you count my broken spirit, my mental health, and my sense of self; they were almost snuffed out, but other than that, I wasn't physically beaten, just in every other way.

Back to the present.

I have wanted to be a writer since I was a child. Books were magical to me. Someone had written the words, and someone else did the illustrations. As a young child, this was beyond anything I could ever imagine.

I was obsessed with books from a very young age. I'd get as many as I possibly could from the library. Books were a welcome escape when chaos and dysfunction enveloped me.

At a young age, I often wrote letters to family members and my dear aunt encouraged me to write more. I started writing other things like stories, my imagination was quite vivid. I'd entertain myself for hours upon hours.

When I became pregnant at just 15 years of age, I faced some critical choices. An abortion, carrying to term and surrendering my child for adoption, or keeping my baby.

To say I was confused and overwhelmed would be a gross understatement. I felt a stirring so strong, that at first, I didn't quite understand what was happening. I was compelled to write, but what would I write about?

It was then I wrote my first poem and scribbled with a frenzy all of my innermost turmoil. I was in a group home and did not have anyone to talk to about this stuff, so my journal became my best friend and confidante.

So, to be told by someone who was supposed to be my partner and biggest supporter that my writing was a waste of time, and that I should be realistic? You may as well claw my heart out and smash it with heavy boots.

This is what HE did repeatedly. Over and over. No support whatsoever. Yet, he wanted me to drop everything and support HIM in whatever new scheme he had his eye on at the moment, but God forbid I have my own passions in life. No, that wasn't allowed or encouraged in any way whatsoever.

My rage festered and grew as I'd ruminate each and every day over my pathetic life. My depression became obvious through rage and despair.

I take ownership in my part of the dysfunction of our relationship. To me though, it was anything but a relationship. More like a dictatorship, where I had no freedom to voice my preferences in how our children should be raised. Most of what I said or did was met with ridicule and or disdain. Oh, and don't forget the silent treatment! Fun times!

As yet, I didn't understand that I was in a relationship with a narcissistic partner. I couldn't win, no matter what I did. I was blamed for damn near everything. He took no accountability for his actions. I mean, hey! Isn't that what women exist for? Take care of everyone and everything, and when life throws shit at ya? You're the fall guy, or gal, to be PC (politically correct).

After all, what the hell did I know about family?! Nothing. According to him, I had no family values to speak of, because I grew up in the foster system from infancy throughout my youth. Not constant, but enough that I never felt safe or knew where I belonged. Anywhere. And now? I didn't even have a place in my own family.

So many questions and no answers. My very life was a looming question mark. How did I come to be at this place in my life?

I had no social life. I missed the company of people. I missed my old life. Most of all, I missed the ballsy quirky me. I wanted out of my tumultuous relationship for years, but I was too scared to leave. Not because I was scared of him, but because I didn't know where to go, or how I'd manage financially. I was completely freaked out, but I couldn't take it anymore.

Last March in 2023, I finally had enough. I made plans to get back to Canada from Egypt. I maxed out my credit card for the airfare and prayed as hard as I could that I would reconnect with family and friends, and hoped I would be welcomed back into their lives again.

I was able to stay with my uncle and his partner in BC and then from there, I stayed with a woman who was my former foster mom from the mid-80s and now I've returned to the home where my oldest son grew up for most of his youth. I'm staying with the family who adopted him. We have since reconnected and found a genuine sense of kinship that has only grown stronger.

I have a job that, for the most part, I enjoy and I'm pretty darn good at, if I may toot my own horn!

Not to say I haven't had moments of doubt, or grief and rage over the last several years, but I feel like I'm finally gaining traction as I make my way in this journey called life.

I've learned a whole shit ton of hard lessons, but how else are you gonna learn, right?! And besides, it's become abundantly clear that I'm a masochist of epic proportions.

Whatever happens from here on out, I know I'm not alone. I have good people by my side, and I believe I will find my True North Strong and Free on my new inner compass with a

lotta help from my friends.

It's only been a little over a year, but I feel confident I'm finding my way in life again.

I often look back to where I was just a year ago. I was completely overwhelmed by everything. Especially grocery stores, since my ex would ridicule everything I bought and tell me I sucked at shopping. Only he could get superior deals. Pfffft...

Guess what?! I don't give a rat's ass what he thinks anymore! Or at the very least, it's not gonna affect me the way it used to.

When I first moved back to Calgary, I rarely went out except for work and a couple of other activities.

Nowadays? I'm rarely home, and I've met many new people from all over. I'm glad it's my home again.

I had lost myself, but now I'm finding a whole new spunky version of me, but I'm older and hopefully a lot wiser than I was. I know what my deal breakers are when it comes to new relationships, and I'm not shy about sharing my opinion in the least.

Except now, I'm calling the shots and I feel like I'm getting to know my true self again.

I rather like who I'm becoming at this stage of my life, but first, I had to take a long hard look in the mirror to see if there were any remaining sparks behind my sad resigned eyes. There was… The woman who was staring back at me told me, "Don't you dare give up. You've come way too far!!"

It's been a long road of self-care and figuring out what really matters in life, and I'm counting my blessings.

Nowadays, when I feel lost or overwhelmed, I look deep into my hazel eyes, and say, "You've got this, girl!"

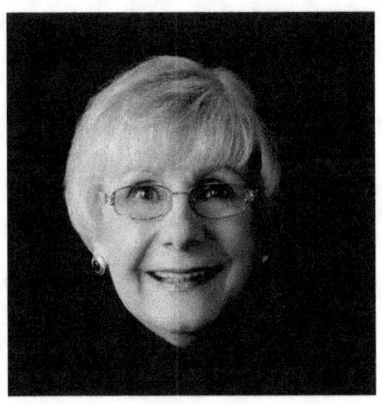

Terri Daunic

Founder and Owner of Distinguished Expressions of Tampa Bay ~

https://www.linkedin.com/in/terri-daunic-13280711/
https://www.facebook.com/terri.daunic
https://www.instagram.com/terridaunic/
https://distinguishedexpressions.biz

Terri Daunic, originally from Columbus, Ohio, has called Tampa, Florida, home for the past 13 years. Settling in South Tampa with her late husband Pierre in 2010, Terri embarked on a diverse professional journey. Her 25-year tenure in State Government, specializing in Criminal Justice Services, fostered a commitment to excellence and community service. Transitioning from government, Terri pursued her passion for portrait photography, establishing a thriving business over 13 years. She refined her craft through training with renowned instructors, earning international awards—a testament to her dedication. Alongside her photography, Terri also serves as a Realtor. Terri's life reflects a pursuit of excellence in public service and artistic expression. Her book offers insights gleaned from these experiences, illuminating a journey shaped by dedication, resilience, and profound connections to community and creativity. Join Terri as she shares her life on thriving in diverse fields, from public service to entrepreneurial pursuits.

Embracing My Future ~ Through Memories Lost in Time

By Terri Daunic

In the memories of your mind there are stairwells you will find; covered with dust, dirt and ashes of another time. It is here you will find buried treasures lost in time.

Sweep you may but the dust lingers every time.

Therefore, go my child and cling to those memories in time.

Before the days of lore there were many who found their true calling in the cobwebs of time.

Run lest you see the true characters and the ruin of time.

Locked away in every room you will find the ancient fear of all men tucked inside a moment of time.

Wrestle you may and fight until the day all the sum of time wrapped in a memory lost in time. Terri A. Daunic –

I was in a dreamlike state before falling asleep one night on October 16th, 2019, and was alarmed at what I was dreaming, and the words that danced through my mind. I decided to get up and write the words as they flowed through my pen and onto paper.

Do I know what these words mean? No, but definitely have been praying about them and how to process them for others. We live in a demanding world full of fear.

I have been thinking about those words for some time. My beloved husband Pierre passed away in July of 2021. After his passing, I was grieving with such pain and I always would go back and read this passage of words.

I believe that as the Bible reads, "We come from dust and we shall go back to dust"

For He Himself knows our frame;

He is mindful that we are *but* dust. Psalm 103:14

"And the Lord God formed man from the dust of the ground." Genesis 2:7

Life is fleeting and we should live it without fear but the full joy of the Lord and all that He has given us.

When my husband passed, he was cremated according to his wishes. I now have his Urn on my stand, where a life well lived, now lives in an Urn as ashes.

Dust, dirt and ashes of another time. All the sum of time wrapped in a memory lost in time.

I believe our childhood traumas and experiences have a profound effect on how we behave as adults. I was raised in fear with a controlling mother. She apologized to me before she passed and told me that was the only way she could control me.

The adversities of my childhood are only a glimmer of struggles throughout my life. I believe that our families were victims of their parents, and, therefore, we are victims of our parents.

These adversities shape our identities, our characters, our thought processes, our mental blocks and our ensuring behaviors and attitudes as adults. I believe these thoughts, beliefs and fears that were instilled in us as young children are the catalyst in our approach to life and may even have traumatic effects on our health and relationships.

My life story is a testimony to strength, courage, and unwavering spirit. I've defied expectations, shattered stereotypes, and embraced life with an unbridled passion. From the rebellious days of my youth to the wisdom of my golden years, I've lived life on my terms. As I pen these memoirs, I hope to inspire others to embrace their own journeys with the same fearlessness and grace. For in the end, it's not about the years we've lived but the life we've created—a life filled with adventure, laughter, and a touch of rebellion.

Beginnings in Small-Town Ohio

My journey began in the heart of Lancaster, Ohio, in 1949. I entered the world as Terri A. Rush, born to Nancy G. Enmen and Richard Rush—a couple whose union was far from ideal. They were young, caught in life's unforgiving grip, struggling to navigate a world fractured by hardship and uncertainty. From the outset, I sensed that my path would be anything but smooth—a realization that would shape my steadfast determination in the years to come.

As a child, I was frequently entrusted to the care of my grandparents and aunts, who provided the stability and love I craved during my mother's absences. My father's presence in my life was fleeting, a mere shadow overshadowed by his own demons. His departure left a void, yet I learned early on to adapt to life's unpredictability—a skill that would serve me well as I embarked on a turbulent journey of self-discovery.

Turmoil and Resilience

Life with my mother was marked by instability and upheaval. As she grappled with her own challenges, I found solace in the warmth of my extended family. Their unwavering support became my anchor amid life's storms, offering a semblance of normalcy in an otherwise tumultuous existence.

My father's absence loomed large, a reminder of the broken nature of my family. His departure and subsequent marriage to another woman only deepened the sense of abandonment I felt. Yet, I refused to be defined by his choices. Instead, I channeled my pain into a fierce determination to forge my own path—a path that would lead me far beyond the confines of Lancaster.

Embracing the Wild Adventure

As I grew older, I embraced the unpredictability of life with open arms. Every twist and turn became an opportunity for growth and self-discovery. I learned to navigate challenges with fierce determination and flexibility, drawing strength from the love and support of those who believed in me.

Despite the turbulence of my early years, I carried within me a strong spirit—a determination to defy the odds and chart my own course. With each passing year, I embraced my identity as a survivor—a woman unafraid to confront life's complexities head-on.

A Life of Triumph

Today, I reflect on my journey with a mixture of gratitude and pride. I am no longer defined by the hardships of my past but empowered by them. I have emerged from the shadows of adversity, as a testimony to the resilience of the human spirit.

My story is a witness to the power of perseverance and self-belief. It is a reminder that our past does not dictate our future—that we have the power to transcend our circumstances and create a life filled with purpose and meaning.

As I look back on my life, I am filled with a profound sense of gratitude for the love and support that carried me through the darkest moments. I am proof that with courage and determination, we can overcome any obstacle and embrace the wild adventure that is life.

Embracing My Journey

Despite the ambiguity surrounding my identity, I refused to be defined by my father's indifference. Instead, I embarked on a journey of self-discovery—an odyssey fueled by Faith and determination.

I found solace in the love of my grandmother and Aunt Jenny, who became my pillars of strength during troubled times. Their nurturing presence offered a sanctuary—a space where I could grow up without fear or judgment.

As I navigated the complexities of adolescence and young adulthood, I learned to accept the mosaic of experiences that shaped me. Each setback and triumph served as a stepping stone toward self-acceptance—a journey marked by courage and introspection.

Finding Wholeness

Today, I stand tall in the light of self-discovery—a woman strengthened by the fires of adversity yet unbroken in spirit. My encounters with my father, though fleeting and bittersweet, taught me invaluable lessons about the fluidity of identity and the resilience of the human heart.

I am no longer defined by the labels imposed upon me by others. Instead, I embrace the fullness of my being—a tapestry woven from the threads of perseverance and authenticity.

In reclaiming my story, I have found wholeness—a sense of belonging that transcends bloodlines and familial ties. I am a testimony to the transformative power of strength and self-love—a woman who, despite her fragmented beginnings, has emerged whole and unapologetically herself.

Finding Resilience in Faith

Following the disheartening encounter with my biological father, I found myself adrift, searching for a sense of purpose and identity. Amidst the uncertainty, I was blessed with the steadfast presence of my Aunt Rene and my Grandmother Effie. Both women were of strong faith and love of God. Grandma Effie and Aunt Rene were true believers and were faithful warriors. Aunt Rene and Grandma Effie always made sure that I was in church, in school, and well-fed. These women of God were strong and an image of what true nurturing angels looked like and they both sought to make a great home for me and my baby brother, Skip, Charlie Morrison.

Aunt Rene and Grandma Effie both became my anchors in the storms, providing stability and structure in a world that often felt chaotic. Raised in a deeply religious household, I was immersed in the rituals and teachings of faith. Each Sunday, Aunt Rene and Grandma Effie would take me to church, where I found solace in the hymns and prayers that echoed through the sanctuary. Both Angels of God were strict but they had caring demeanors that nurtured me with discipline and love, instilling values that would shape my character for years to come.

Despite the challenges of my upbringing, I never lacked for anything under the guidance of Grandma Effie and Aunt Rene's care. Both of these ladies from heaven had culinary skills that filled our home with the aroma of home-cooked meals every day and that created a sense of warmth and belonging amidst the turmoil.

A New Chapter with Cecil Terrance Floyd

Amidst the turbulence of my childhood, my mother's life took an unexpected turn when she met Cecil Terrance Floyd—known affectionately as Cecil or Terry or CT—at Stone's Bar and Grill, where she worked as a bartender. CT was a military man of strong character and resilience, a stark contrast to the instability that had defined my early years.

CT brought structure and discipline into our lives, reflecting the regimented lifestyle of the military. His presence offered a sense of security—a departure from the uncertainty that had plagued us before. As I observed his unwavering commitment to duty and honor, I began to appreciate the virtues of working hard for anything I wanted in life with perseverance.

The Journey Continues

As I navigated the complexities of adolescence and young adulthood under the watchful eyes of Aunt Rene and CT, I discovered my own reservoirs of strength and resilience. Their strong faith and discipline became the bedrock upon which I built my identity.

The lessons learned from Aunt Rene's strict yet nurturing upbringing and CT's disciplined approach to life shaped my worldview and instilled within me a sense of purpose. I began to understand that true identity transcends biological ties—it is made through experiences, values, and the faith that sustains us through life's trials.

Gratitude and Growth

Today, I reflect on my journey with a profound sense of thankfulness for the strong women and resilient men who shaped my path. Their faith and enduring love carried me through the darkest moments, teaching me invaluable lessons about resilience, courage, and the transformative power of faith.

As I embrace the fullness of my identity, I carry with me the indelible imprint of Aunt Rene's nurturing spirit and CT's unwavering strength. Their presence in my life continues to inspire me to live authentically and fearlessly, knowing that true strength lies not in avoiding hardships but in working through them with   strong faith and lots of strength.

Life on the Move

The marriage of my mother and CT marked the beginning of a new chapter—one defined by constant change and adventure. CT's career as a Radar Instructor with the U.S. Air Force meant that we would be moving to various military bases, each stop offering a unique glimpse into a different way of life.

As a child navigating the transient nature of military life, I quickly adapted to the rhythm of change. Packing up our belongings and relocating became routine, transforming me into a seasoned traveler at a young age. Each new base presented opportunities for growth and discovery, exposing me to diverse cultures and perspectives.

Living on remote sites with CT's work was always a work in progress, creating new friends, attending new schools, and creating a family home while learning the tapestry in our new environment. We learned to lean on each other during deployments and separations, drawing strength from the bonds created by our shared experiences. Tensions were high while living in various Air Force assignments. One way or the other we made it through.

Embracing Military Values

The military lifestyle instilled in me a deep appreciation for discipline, structure, and strength. CT's role as a Radar Instructor demanded precision and dedication—values that permeated every aspect of our daily lives.

Under CT's guidance, I learned the importance of adaptability and perseverance in the face of adversity. His commitment to duty and honor left an indelible mark on my character, shaping me into a person of integrity and determination.

As we traversed the landscapes of various military bases, I embraced the ethos of service and sacrifice. Our lives were intertwined with the larger tapestry of the U.S. Air Force community—a community defined by mutual support, friendship, and character.

Lessons Learned

The nomadic lifestyle of military families taught me invaluable lessons about resilience and flexibility. Each new base brought its own set of challenges and opportunities, pushing me to accept change with an open heart and mind.

Amidst the transient nature of our existence, I discovered the beauty of making connections and leaving a positive impact wherever life took us. The friendships made in military communities became a source of strength and solidarity, grounding me in a world defined by constant flux.

Grateful for the Journey

Today, I look back on my military upbringing with profound gratitude. The nomadic lifestyle molded me into a person of strength and empathy, equipping me with the tools to navigate life's ever-changing landscapes.

As I carry forward the values instilled in me by CT and the U.S. Air Force community, I remain committed to accepting life's adventures with courage and fortitude. My journey as a military child has shaped not only my identity but also my worldview, reminding me of the profound impact of service, sacrifice, and unwavering dedication to a greater purpose.

The Blue Dress

During a visit back to Lancaster, a significant moment unfolded—an encounter with my real father, Richard Rush. This encounter, albeit brief, held a special significance as Richard made an effort to connect with me, his daughter. As a young girl, I cherished the moments spent with him, especially when he took me shopping.

In a store window, I laid eyes on a beautiful blue dress that captured my heart. I was enchanted by its elegance and imagined myself adorned in its splendor. Richard, unable to purchase the dress at that moment, promised to buy it for me later and send it to me. His gesture left a lasting impression, a glimmer of hope that perhaps our fractured relationship could mend.

Blended Family Dynamics

Amidst the backdrop of my mother's marriage to CT and our nomadic military lifestyle, our family expanded with the addition of three siblings—Joni, Mark, and Joel. CT and my mother created a hectic household filled with the challenges of raising a growing and blended family.

Before CT, my mother was briefly married to Charlie Morrison, a man whom I adored as a father figure and mentor during our time in Bossier City, Louisiana. Charlie and my mother welcomed a baby boy named Charles Morrison, aka Skip, adding another layer to our family dynamics.

We left Biloxi, Mississippi, and moved to Rockville, Indiana along with my extended family. The blended family structure was a new experience in my upbringing, teaching me the values of unity and strength amidst a life of everchanging upheavals marred by a Military life.

The Promise Unfulfilled

The anticipation of receiving the blue dress promised by my real father, Richard Rush, became a symbol of hope and longing during my childhood in Rockville, Indiana. Each day, I awaited the mailman's arrival with eager expectation, yearning to unwrap the cherished gift that would bridge the divide between us.

As days turned into weeks, the mailbox became a place of both anticipation and disappointment. I clung to the belief that Richard would honor his promise, unaware of the complexities that overshadowed our fractured relationship. My mother's attempts to shield me from the harsh reality only fueled my determination to hold onto faith.

Amidst the countryside backdrop of our farm   house, I grappled with the conflicting emotions of hope and disillusionment. The blue dress embodied more than just a material possession—it symbolized the desire for connection and validation from a father figure who remained elusive.

Lessons in Resilience

The unfulfilled promise of the blue dress taught me invaluable lessons about undiscovered internal strength and the complexities of human relationships. Through tears and heartache, I discovered the fragility of trust and the importance of confronting harsh truths with courage. To this day, I lean on my Faith in God knowing there is always something better for me to obtain. I set goals on a daily basis to become a better version of myself.

My mother's candid revelations about Richard's limitations served as a catalyst for growth, challenging me to navigate disappointment with fortitude and understanding. It taught me to never rely on anyone, as my own strength and God's Favor are enough to carry me through. As I processed the disappointment, I began to cultivate a deeper sense of self-reliance and inner strength that I carry to this day. It's not one and done, it is something I have to do every day and it only gets better with time.

The blue dress, once a beacon of hope, became a constant reminder of the complexities of parental love and the inherent imperfections of human connections. In

In its absence, I discovered the power of flexibility—a quality that would accompany me throughout life's unpredictable journey.

Healing and Self-Discovery

Today, I reflect on the unfulfilled promise of the blue dress with a sense of compassion and understanding. The innocence of childhood gave way to the wisdom of adulthood, transforming disappointment into an opportunity for introspection and healing.

The journey from anticipation to acceptance taught me that true strength is found through adversity. I no longer seek validation from external sources but embrace the power that resides within—a strength nurtured by the trials and tribulations of life's unfolding narrative in a well-blended family of mixed emotions, high anxiety, and turmoil.

As I continue to navigate life's complexities, I carry with me the ever growing lessons of hope, Faith in God, and self-discovery. The unfulfilled promise of the blue dress remains a reminder of the transformative power of embracing life's uncertainties with an open heart and pushing on even when we don't know what is around the next turn in life.

The Gift of Love

The day I found a package in the mailbox, containing a beautiful blue dress, remains etched in my memory as a profound moment of joy and realization. As I eagerly unwrapped the gift, my heart swelled with excitement and delight. Here was proof, tangible and undeniable, that I was loved and cherished.

In that fleeting moment of triumph, I rushed to share my newfound conviction with my mother. I proclaimed that she had been wrong about my real father, convinced that his gesture of sending the blue dress was a testament to his love for me.

However, life has a way of unraveling our expectations and revealing deeper truths. Unbeknownst to me, my stepfather, CT, had witnessed my daily wait at the mailbox and was moved to action. In a touching display of love and compassion, CT had gone out and purchased the blue dress that brought me such joy.

I clung to that blue dress for years and never thought how it really shaped my life. So much that I created a "portrait" of a beautiful woman in the Blue Dress that hangs in my home to this day.

I am also a professional portrait artist and photographer. I created this piece of art to be a testament to the human spirit of yearning for love and connection in all of us. Our trust in our parent's love and meaning in life, that what we always want is never the answer to life's adventure in becoming who we really are.

Lessons in Unexpected Love

The revelation of CT's thoughtful gesture years later was a poignant reminder of the transformative power of unexpected love. CT's quiet act of kindness transcended the complexities of familial ties, leaving an indelible imprint on my heart.

Through CT's selfless gesture, I learned that love is not bound by bloodlines or biological connections. It is a force that transcends circumstances, revealing itself in the most unexpected ways.

The blue dress became a symbol of the love and devotion that CT showered upon our family—a love that was steadfast and unwavering, even in the face of life's uncertainties. His silent support and unwavering presence shaped my understanding of parental love and the enduring bonds of family.

Gratitude and Reflection

Today, I carry forward the lessons learned from CT's profound act of love. The blue dress serves as a poignant reminder of the depth of human connection and the transformative power of unexpected kindness.

As I reflect on the tapestry of my life, I am filled with gratitude for the love and support that has guided me through adversity. CT's legacy lives on in the lessons of resilience, compassion, and unconditional love—a testament to the profound impact of genuine human connection, even though it is not perceived as love at the time.

May we all be inspired to embrace life's obstacles with courage and grace, guided by the enduring spirit of unexpected love that illuminates our path.

A Life of Constant Change

My childhood was marked by perpetual movement and change, a result of my family's military lifestyle. Over the years, we traversed the vast expanse of 17 different states, with me attending a new school nearly every year or two. This transient existence shaped my academic journey, leaving me oscillating between being academically ahead or lagging behind.

Despite the challenges of constant relocation, I embraced the opportunity to forge new friendships and maintain connections with old friends from my nomadic school years. Each new school brought a fresh set of experiences and challenges, contributing to my resilience and adaptability.

In 1966, our family received orders to relocate from Indiana, where we had resided since 1964, to the picturesque coastal town of Cambria, California. It was a welcome change from the cold Midwest to the sunny California beach! This move marked my sophomore and junior years of high school, during which I attended Coast High School nestled in the hills just below Hearst Castle. Hearst Castle, the majestic palace of William Randolph Hearst from the Hearst Media Empire, served as a backdrop to my transformative years in Cambria, California. In this picturesque coastal town, I not only experienced the beauty of the ocean and the enchantment of daily life but also learned how to drive a "4 on the floor" on the roads behind the castle.

Each day after school, we boarded a bus to nearby Cayucos, crossing the world-famous Davies Bridge while tunes like Sonny and Cher's "I Got You Babe" or the Boxtops' "The Letter" played in the background. The views of the Pacific Ocean and migrating whales along the coastline made these daily commutes a dreamlike experience.

Cambria was a place of many firsts for me—my first boyfriend, my first kiss, and my first car, a 1964 Corvair! Our home was situated below a hillside, facing the Pacific Ocean. We could hear the waves crashing at night during dinner, creating a truly magical atmosphere.

I also began working at the Cambria Pines Lodge as a maid, where many celebrities sought respite from the L.A. lifestyle. I distinctly remember cleaning Jerry Lewis's room after his stay; finding his socks and toothbrush left behind became cherished souvenirs of an encounter with a great movie star of the day.

The idyllic days were spent in Cambria, where each moment was filled with wonder, music, and the endless beauty of California's central coastline.

We then received orders to move from sunny California to the brutal cold of Goose Bay, Labrador.

Goose Bay, Labrador - A Military Adventure

Amidst the whirlwind of change, my junior and senior years unfolded in the remote and frigid landscape of Goose Bay, Labrador. Nestled within a Strategic Air Command (SAC) Air Base, Goose Bay served as a testimony to the military-centric lifestyle that defined my upbringing.

Living in Goose Bay was an adventure of its own, characterized by the isolation and camaraderie unique to military bases. The air command center buzzed with activity, offering a glimpse into the intricate workings of national defense.

Despite the desolate surroundings, I found solace in the familiarity of routine and the bonds created within the tight-knit community. Goose Bay became more than just a backdrop—it was a place of growth and transition, culminating in my high school graduation.

Graduation and Reflection

The culmination of my high school years in Goose Bay marked a significant milestone—a testament to my resilience and adaptability amidst life's constant flux. Graduating amidst the backdrop of a military base instilled within me a profound sense of pride and gratitude for the experiences that shaped my journey.

As I reflect on my nomadic upbringing and the challenges of navigating multiple schools and environments, I am grateful for the lessons learned and the friendships made along the way. Each chapter of my life, from the bustling cities of the United States to the remote landscapes of Labrador, contributed to the tapestry of my identity.

Embracing Life's Adventures

Today, I carry forward the spirit of steadfast determination and adaptability instilled in me by my nomadic upbringing. The memories of Goose Bay and the myriad other places I called home serve as a witness to the transformative power of embracing life's adventures with an open heart and Faith in God.

As I continue to navigate life's complexities, I am grateful for the lessons learned and the connections made along the way. My journey is a Faith-filled journey and a witness to the strength and power of the human spirit and the enduring bonds that transcend geographical boundaries.

May we all embrace life's adventures with courage and grace, knowing that every experience contributes to the fabric of our existence and shapes the narrative of our lives.

After leaving the cold wilderness of Goose Bay, Labrador we traveled back to the United States in 1969-1970 to Chillicothe, Ohio.

Life Encounters and Near Death Experiences

In the summer of 1975, a routine lunch outing turned into a heart-stopping ordeal for me. As I pulled into Burger Boy Foodarama with my friends, the tranquility of the day was shattered with the sound of gunfire. Trapped in my car amidst the chaos of a random shooting, I found myself facing mortality head-on. Miraculously spared from harm by mere inches, I emerged from this harrowing experience with a renewed perspective on life's fragility and the strength of the human spirit. Join me on a gripping journey of survival, courage, and the enduring power of hope in the face of unexpected adversity.

Being shot at is the most terrifying experience in a person's life, especially when you cannot see the shooter or know where the shots are coming from. This day was the most horrific day for me. I prayed to God for help while a storm of bullets sprayed down on unsuspecting victims.

The police finally showed up to counterattack the active shooter who was hidden on the grassy hill above the shopping center. We were finally brought into safety by the SWAT Team that had surrounded us during gunfire.

The woman in front of me was shot, as was the woman directly behind me. The police officer told me that the only thing that saved my life was the banner that was hung over the drive-through. I was told that had the shooter stepped only one foot to his left, he would have been able to shoot me in the head with his 30.6 caliber rifle. Again, the police officer reiterated that I either had good luck or someone was watching over me. I should have been shot that day and killed, but I know God was with me as He has been and always will be.

My life story is a testimony to trials, tribulation, courage, and an unwavering spirit of faith. I've defied expectations, shattered stereotypes, and embraced life with an unbridled passion. From the rebellious days of my youth to the wisdom of my golden years, I've lived life on my terms. As I pen these memoirs, I hope to inspire others to embrace their own journeys with the same fearlessness and grace. For in the end, it's not about the years we've lived but the life we've created—a life filled with adventure, laughter, and a touch of rebellion.

End Result: Keep on going no matter what has happened, because life truly is a process not a "destination" ~ Create Your Own Life....You have the eraser, if you don't like how your life is going, then erase it and start over with a fresh canvas. – In the service of many, you will find your calling.

As the saying goes, "If you find yourself driving through Hell…Keep on going"!

Driving Head-on into Life

In the summer of 1973, I faced a brush with fate that forever changed my outlook on life. While I was driving my cherished 1968 SS Camaro, a routine journey to pick up my daughter, Sonya took a terrifying turn. I was confronted by a semi-truck blocking my path, I braced for impact, my world spinning into chaos.

Miraculously surviving a catastrophic collision that defied explanation, I emerged from the wreckage with renewed resilience and gratitude. Each day became a testament to the preciousness of life and the enduring power of hope.

Join me on a gripping journey of survival and introspection as I navigate the aftermath of near-tragedy and discover the true meaning of embracing life's journey with courage and gratitude.

This memoir is a compelling reminder that every moment is a gift, and every challenge is an opportunity to embrace the resilience of the human spirit.

I was driving early in the morning from Chillicothe, Ohio, to Lancaster, Ohio in the Summer of 1973.

I had just geared up and was heading down the highway, not looking for adventure, but I found it quickly.

I had just sped up to 75 miles per hour on this stretch of highway heading North and noticed two cars in front of me and a semi in the Southbound lane, awaiting a left-hand turn onto an overpass. I turned on the radio, and picked up a cigarette, lit it, and looked back at traffic. The two cars in front of me had disappeared, and the semi now covered the northbound lanes as it headed to the overpass. There was no way to escape hitting the semi head-on, so I slammed on the brakes and turned the steering wheel, hoping to drive into the nearby open space. It was too late, for all options were gone. I was moving sideways with the tires smoking as I placed all of my weight on the brakes... all 99 pounds of me.

I prayed, Oh God, Help Me! And, He did... I made impact with the semi which had a full 500-gallon gas tank, and the rear end of the Camino was being pulled under the tractor trailer. I finally made contact with the semi and screamed for my life. The driver of the Semi came running to me. My car was totaled, and I was in shock and amazed that I was still alive, as was the driver who was trying to get me out of the car.

A police officer was there within minutes. The police officer said you must have someone looking over you...You should have been killed on impact as the driver had just filled the 500-gallon gas tank on the semi. Yes, I do have someone looking over me, and He is God with all of His Angels. We are spared from tragic accidents because He has a job for us to do, and we have not yet fulfilled our Purpose on this Earth.

In the summer of 1978, I faced another life-threatening ordeal during childbirth that would test my resilience and faith. As I labored in the hospital, a series of medical mishaps unfolded, leaving me with life-threatening complications after the birth of my son, Richard.

Surviving the Shadows: A Mother's Journey Through Life and Near Death Experience

May 8th, 1978, was supposed to be a day of new beginnings—a day to welcome my son Richard into the world. Little did I know it would become a harrowing ordeal that brought me to the brink of death.

The night before Richard's birth, I found myself in the throes of labor at the hospital. Hours passed, and I awaited the arrival of my precious child amidst the chaos of a busy maternity ward. The only doctor on call was juggling deliveries, rushing between my room and another expectant mother's.

As the pivotal moment arrived, the doctor performed a high-forceps delivery, but amidst the frenzy, he inadvertently left afterbirth in my uterus—a fateful oversight that would soon unleash a cascade of life-threatening events.

After returning home with my newborn son, a mysterious odor permeated the air. Within days, I began passing alarming blood clots, a silent harbinger of the impending crisis. Ignored by medical advice to rest, I found myself descending into a terrifying spiral of hemorrhage and despair.

In a blur of panic, I summoned all my strength to signal for help, desperately trying to avert disaster. It was a race against time as I teetered on the brink of unconsciousness, grappling with the stark reality of imminent death. I could feel life leaving my body as blood left my body like a faucet that had been turned on.

The arrival of emergency responders marked a frenzied chapter in my fight for survival. Transported to the hospital in a hearse due to a shortage of ambulances, I clung to life as medical personnel battled to stabilize my failing body.

Amidst the chaos of the emergency room, I experienced a surreal calmness—a transcendent moment of surrender and prayer. As my life hung in the balance, I beseeched the divine for a chance to see another day, to feel warmth return to my cold, fragile body. I could feel the descending white cloud hovering over my body as I lay frozen in calmness. The cloud seemed to move closer to me and pull my breath away. I could hear the medical personnel as they fought to restore my blood pressure, which was dropping by 5 points very quickly. I could hear the attending nurse shouting to the doctors that they were losing me. I began to pray that as much as my blood pressure was dropping, it would rise as much if I were to remain with the living.

In a dramatic turn, my blood pressure began to rise, a glimmer of hope amidst the looming darkness. Urgently whisked into surgery, I was propelled down hospital corridors, clinging to the fragile thread of life, my fate entrusted to the hands of tireless medical professionals.

The medical personnel that drove me to the hospital came to visit me afterward. And, again, I heard the promise of God through the words spoken to me that day. "After 25 years as a paramedic, I have never seen anyone lose as much blood as you did and live to tell about it !   Someone must have been with you…dust, dirt, and ashes of another time, wrapped up in a moment in time. Today, my son Richard is doing very well and is 47 years old.

Beyond Rebellion: Memoirs of a Badass Classy Woman

The swinging 60s, 70s, 80s, and 90s. A time of rebellion and change. I was young and restless, eager to break free from the conventional norms that stifled my spirit. Growing up in the midst of social upheaval, I found myself caught between the innocence of youth and the allure of the world and all it had to offer.

A Wild Ride Through the Decade of Decadence

As the 70s dawned, I shed my flower-child persona and embraced the disco scene. Life became a kaleidoscope of daring adventures. I navigated the disco balls and bell-bottoms with style, making my mark in a world, or so I thought.

Today, I look back on my life with a mixture of nostalgia and pride. I survived the tumultuous decades, emerging stronger and wiser. The lessons I've learned along the way have shaped me into the badass, classy woman I am today. I've seen it all—the highs, the lows, and everything in between. Through it all, I've remained true to myself, never compromising my values or losing sight of my dreams.

I stand tall in the light of self-discovery—a woman forged by the fires of adversity yet unbroken in spirit. My encounters with my father, though fleeting and bittersweet, taught me invaluable lessons about the value of my identity and steadfast belief in God and   the human heart.

I am no longer defined by the labels imposed upon me by others. Instead, I embrace the fullness of my being—a tapestry woven from the threads of my struggles, perseverance, steadfast authenticity, and belief in myself as a human being, a woman, a mother, and that you have to be badass to make it through this world.

In reclaiming my narrative, I have found wholeness—a sense of belonging that transcends bloodlines and familial ties. I am a testament to the transformative power of resilience and self-love—a woman who, despite her fragmented beginnings, has emerged whole and unapologetically herself.

I retired from working for the Criminal Justice System in 2010 after 25 years of service and relocated to Tampa, Florida. I am the owner of Distinguished Expressions of Tampa Bay, a professional portrait studio. I am also a Real Estate Agent working with Coldwell Banker in South Tampa, Florida. I am now 75 years old and I am "just beginning" my new life in excellent health and wealth!

JOIN THE MOVEMENT!
#BAUW

Becoming An Unstoppable Woman
With She Rises Studios

She Rises Studios was founded by Hanna Olivas and Adriana Luna Carlos, the mother-daughter duo, in mid-2020 as they saw a need to help empower women worldwide. They are the podcast hosts of the *She Rises Studios Podcast* and Amazon best-selling authors and motivational speakers who travel the world. Hanna and Adriana are the movement creators of #BAUW - Becoming An Unstoppable Woman: The movement has been created to universally impact women of all ages, at whatever stage of life, to overcome insecurities, and adversities, and develop an unstoppable mindset. She Rises Studios educates, celebrates, and empowers women globally.

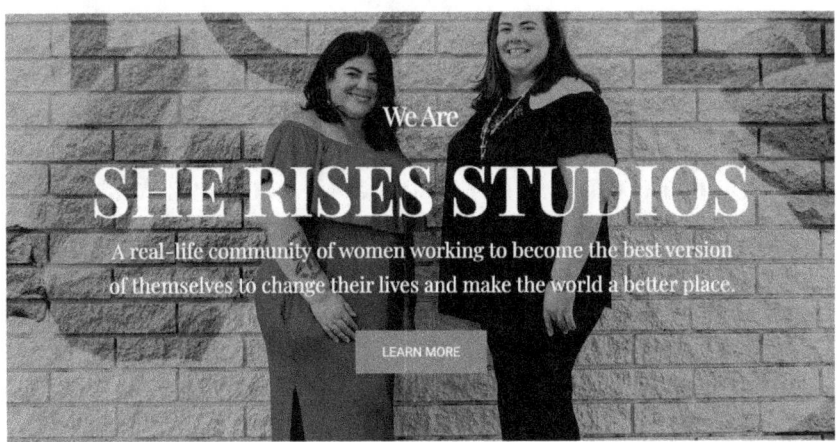

Looking to Join Us in our Next Anthology

or Publish YOUR Own?

She Rises Studios Publishing offers full-service publishing, marketing, book tour, and campaign services. For more information,

contact info@sherisesstudios.com

We are always looking for women who want to share their stories and expertise and feature their businesses on our podcasts, in our books, and in our magazines.

SEE WHAT WE DO

OUR PODCAST   **OUR BOOKS**   **OUR SERVICES**

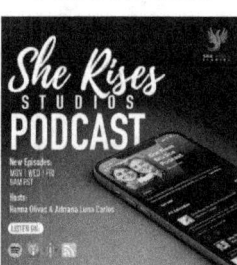 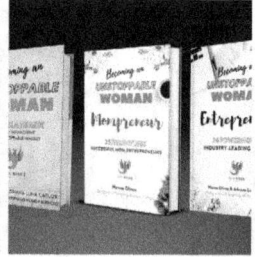 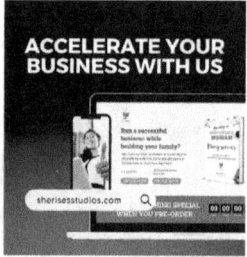

Be featured in the Becoming An Unstoppable Woman magazine, published in 13 countries and sold in all major retailers. Get the visibility you need to LEVEL UP in your business!

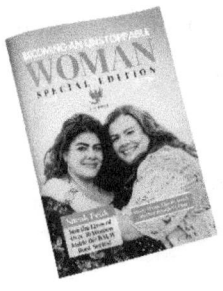 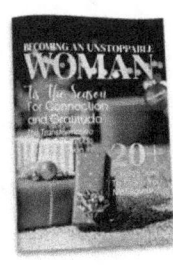 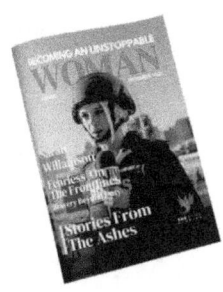

Have your own TV show streamed across major platforms like Roku TV, Amazon Fire Stick, Apple TV and more!

Learn to leverage your expertise. Build your online presence and grow your audience with FENIX TV.
https://fenixtv.sherisesstudios.com/

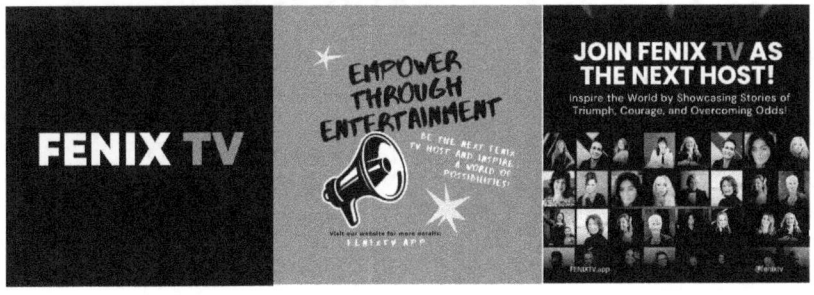

Visit www.SheRisesStudios.com to see how YOU can join the #BAUW movement and help your community to achieve the UNSTOPPABLE mindset.

Have you checked out the *She Rises Studios Podcast?*

Find us on all MAJOR platforms: Spotify, IHeartRadio, Apple Podcasts, Google Podcasts, etc.

Looking to become a sponsor or build a partnership?

Email us at info@sherisesstudios.com

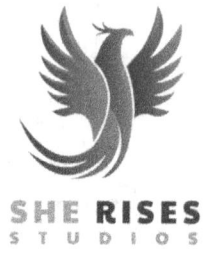